WITH KARIN STEINBACH

TRANSLATED BY BILLI BIERLING
AFTERWORD BY STEVE HOUSE

UELI STECK
MY LIFE IN CLIMBING

A LEGENDS AND LORE TITLE

MOUNTAINEERS
BOOKS

MOUNTAINEERS BOOKS is the publishing division of The Mountaineers, an organization founded in 1906 and dedicated to the exploration, preservation, and enjoyment of outdoor and wilderness areas.

1001 SW Klickitat Way, Suite 201 • Seattle, WA 98134
800.553.4453 • www.mountaineersbooks.org

Originally published as *Der nächste Schritt*
© 2016 by Piper Verlag GmbH, München/Berlin, published under the imprint Malik

Translation copyright © 2018 by Billi Bierling
Afterword copyright © 2018 by Steve House

Printed in the United States of America
Distributed in the United Kingdom by Cordee, www.cordee.co.uk
21 20 19 18   1 2 3 4 5

Copyeditor: Chris Dodge
Design and layout: Heidi Smets
Cover photograph: *Ueli Steck* (Photo by PatitucciPhoto)

Library of Congress Cataloging-in-Publication Data
Names: Steck, Ueli, author. | Steinbach, Karin, author. | Bierling, Billi, translator.
Title: Ueli Steck : my life in climbing / by Ueli Steck, with Karin Steinbach; translated by Billi Bierling.
Description: Seattle, Washington: Mountaineers Books, [2018] | Series: Legends and Lore Series | "Originally published as Der nachste Schritt
   2016 by Piper Verlag GmbH, Munchen/Berlin, published under the imprint   Malik"-- T.p. verso.
Identifiers: LCCN 2017040143| ISBN 9781680511321 (pbk) | ISBN 9781680511338 (ebook)
Subjects: LCSH: Steck, Ueli. | Mountaineers--Switzerland--Biography.
Classification: LCC GV199.92.S73 S74 2018 | DDC 796.522092 [B] --dc23
LC record available at https://lccn.loc.gov/2017040143

Mountaineers Books titles may be purchased for corporate, educational, or other promotional sales, and our authors are available for a wide range of events. For information on special discounts or booking an author, contact our customer service at 800-553-4453 or mbooks@mountaineersbooks.org.

♻ Printed on recycled paper

ISBN (paperback): 978-1-68051-132-1
ISBN (ebook): 978-1-68051-133-8

CONTENTS

EVEREST
WHEN THE WORLD
SUDDENLY CHANGES

The highest mountain in the world is immensely attractive to a lot of people, and so it was for me. When I started to discover the challenges of high-altitude mountaineering at the beginning of the new millennium, I was unable to escape its fascination. During my first Everest attempt, from the north side in Tibet in 2011, I made it to about 100 meters below the summit. But when I stopped feeling my toes, I immediately turned back since I did not want to risk getting frostbite. A year later I reached the summit with my Nepali climbing partner Tenji via the normal route, on the south side, in Nepal. Despite the fact that I had climbed without supplemental oxygen, some people wondered what on earth I was doing on a heavily trodden path on an over-crowded mountain.

The answer was easy: Mount Everest offers a range of attractive routes and possible projects, but before I could even think about doing a technically challenging ascent, I needed to find out what to expect up there and how strong my body would be at an elevation of 8848 meters. The 2012 ascent went smoothly, and I acclimatized very well. This encouraged me to plan a more challenging route for the following season. It did not have to be the Horseshoe—the traverse from Nuptse via Lhotse to Everest that had long been an unsolved climbing challenge. I hatched a more modest plan for spring 2013: an Everest–Lhotse traverse with my British friend Jonathan Griffith, who had lived in Chamonix in the French Alps for many years, and Italian climber Simone Moro, who is best known for his winter ascents of 8000-meter peaks.

Jon and I flew to the Nepalese capital, Kathmandu, at the end of March with Peter Fanconi and his friend Juan. The pair was going to accompany us to Everest Base Camp and then trek back on their own. Simone had already been in Nepal working as a helicopter pilot, and we had made arrangements to meet en route. As is frequently the case, we had to wait at the Kathmandu airport for our flight to Lukla. Small planes usually depart from Kathmandu only in the early morning, and if fog or clouds impair visibility, then all flights are canceled. As soon as the weather is good enough for the planes to fly, mayhem usually breaks out.

In Lukla, at 2860 meters, Twin Otter planes land in quick succession at an airstrip that is just 527 meters long. Immediately after touchdown, which is usually a bit rough, the pilots have to hit the brakes hard to avoid crashing into the wall, which seems to rapidly move closer. At the front of the airstrip, a cliff drops about 600 meters down toward the Dudh Khosi River. Once the airplanes have landed, it's pandemonium. People want to retrieve their bags as quickly as possible because mix-ups can happen: Porters have been known to walk off with the wrong luggage.

As I had been to Nepal a few times before, I was not really fazed and was looking forward to trekking through the Khumbu. Since my first visit in 2001, I have always enjoyed coming back here. The region has somehow touched my heart. One can wander from lodge to lodge and enjoy the stunning views of snow-covered peaks rising up from the barren valley. The trails are very well maintained since thousands of people visit this beautiful region every year. We had picked a pretty quiet time. The main trekking season is traditionally fall, when thousands of visitors stomp through the valley, but tourism dropped after the devastating earthquake in the spring of 2015.

The first trekking stage took us from Lukla to Namche Bazaar, which, at 3440 meters, is considered the gateway to the real Himalaya. From here the peaks soar high into the sky. Since Base Camp lies 1600 meters higher, to avoid altitude-related headaches we took our time and had a rest day in Pangboche. In the morning we visited the local monastery and joined a Buddhist ceremony. Appeasement of the gods—*puja*—is an important part of every expedition. Jon wasn't feeling well after the food he had eaten the previous day, but he was good-humored even though he had spent much of the night on the toilet. This is part of traveling in the Himalaya.

After our visit to the monastery, we continued to Dingboche (4500 meters), where we intended to stay for a couple of nights. Farther up the valley, one trail continues toward Mount Everest and the other one veers off to the Chukung Valley, which is closed in by the 5845-meter Amphu Laptsa Pass leading to the Makalu Valley. Instead of resting I made the most of my day by going for a run up the valley all the way to Chukung, from which I dashed up Chukung Ri, a 5546-meter summit.

After this beautiful start to our expedition, we trekked from Dingboche north to Lobuche, where we met Simone the following day. Now the team was complete, and slowly but surely we trekked to Base Camp, finally reaching it on April 11. Calling it a camp is something of an understatement, as it has become practically a city nestled in the mountains at 5300 meters. Every year various operators set up their tents on the moraine of the glacier, and yaks and porters carry tons of gear up the valley. During the climbing season around 1500 climbers, Sherpas, and expedition staff members call this their temporary home.

I was very excited and found it hard to hold back and not start out toward Everest immediately. I guess this is why I ran up to Camp 1 on the day after our arrival. At an elevation of 6100 meters, Camp 1 lies in the Valley of Silence, a labyrinth of ice towers and deep crevasses just above the Khumbu Icefall. Every year, the Icefall Doctors prepare a suitable way through this crazy maze of crevasses, using ropes and ladders. In order to finance the work of the Icefall Doctors, every expedition pays a fee in addition to that paid for the climbing permit. It is a risky job since the icefall contains many dangers, which have killed not only Sherpas but also western clients. In April 2014 an avalanche killed sixteen Sherpas while they were preparing the icefall for climbers.

I had brought a pair of running shoes with spikes and was excited to be able to run through the prepared icefall. The shoes passed the test, proving much easier to run in than heavy mountaineering boots. The 800 meters up to Camp 1 were pretty effortless for me. After two days at Base Camp, we bid goodbye to Juan and Peter, who were trekking back to Lukla. But for Jon, Simone, and me the expedition was now getting more serious, and we had to start with proper acclimatization. On April 14 we went up to Camp 2 and descended to Base Camp the same day. Two days later Simone and I carried some gear to Camp 2 and stayed up there. The weather was favorable, and we were making good progress. For the time being we were the only Western climbers at Camp 2, where Sherpas were still busy setting up tents for the clients. That evening they invited us for dinner. Of course we had *dal bhat*, the traditional Nepali dish of rice and lentils, which at an elevation of 6500 meters seems like haute cuisine. Once again I was impressed by the infrastructure that had been carried up to this elevation. To me, the Sherpa mess tent, where we had dinner, was pretty luxurious, but it was nothing compared to the plush mess tents for members of the commercial expeditions.

While the Sherpas continued to pitch tents the next morning, Simone and I went on a reconnaissance mission toward Everest's West Shoulder to check out the conditions up there. Our plan was to reach the West Shoulder from Camp 2, climb to the summit via the Hornbein Couloir on the north side, descend via the South Col, and continue to Lhotse—a traverse from the highest to the fourth-highest mountain in the world. The previous year, when I was on the south side of Everest, two American teams had attempted the route through the Hornbein Couloir. However, after spending a month fixing ropes, they did not reach even the West Shoulder. I could hardly wait to find out what we could expect.

It was already pretty warm when we headed out, and very soon we encountered rocky terrain. The climbing was not very hard, but the rock was quite loose in places, and we had to be careful. As we were climbing without a rope, we moved quite quickly, and although we had not been at altitude for long, it was surprisingly easy. When we reached 6900 meters Simone had had enough and turned back, but I continued up on my own. I was so excited to find out how steep and difficult it would be higher up and what the conditions would be like. The technical difficulties seemed pretty reasonable to me. A few steep parts turned out to be sheer ice, and while overcoming them was strenuous exercise, the climbing was not too demanding.

After a while I started to feel the effects of altitude. I was no longer making such good progress, afternoon clouds were moving in, and it was getting cold. I checked my altimeter, which indicated 7200 meters, and put on my down mittens. The top of the West Shoulder was not that much farther, and I was keen to reach it. I was hoping to catch a glimpse of the North Face, from which we would climb the Hornbein Couloir on our way to the summit. Engulfed in clouds, I continued. It was still early, and I had plenty of time. Up here the ice was covered in snow, which made climbing a little less strenuous and safer. Finally I stepped out of the gully and was standing atop the West Shoulder.

By now, however, the clouds had reduced visibility to about 10 meters. For a moment I was disappointed that I had been denied the view of the North Face I had so longed to see. I climbed up higher to check out the snow conditions and found the hard snow cover was perfect for kicking steps. Unbelievable! This is just what we would need for the summit push. I was already imagining how we would set out from there, leave our tents, and move toward the summit following the light of our headlamps.

Time to stop dreaming. Hungry, I started my descent, securing the most difficult parts with an old fixed rope that had been left behind by earlier expeditions. This would aid us when we carried up tents and sleeping bags. I reached Camp 2 just as it was getting dark. This time we had to cook our own dinner, and we decided on Swiss rösti—a dish of fried grated potatoes. Shortly after eating I fell asleep, content. After having been at Base Camp for only six days, I had already reached 7500 meters. I had climbed higher in six days than the Americans had done in four weeks the previous year.

After spending two more nights at Camp 2 for acclimatization, Simone and I returned to Base Camp. We were on track: we felt really well, the conditions on the mountain were superb, and we were extremely motivated. All doubts troubling us before the expedition were gone. The many factors we had considered again and again during preparation that might lead to failure had suddenly disappeared. I had already ascended to the West Shoulder, and the route had proved unproblematic. Our team got on very well, and we were all pulling in the same direction. Everything seemed perfect.

Then the weather turned bad, and we decided to stay at Base Camp and rest for a few days. There was nothing to do but wait.

▲ ▲ ▲

In addition to climbing big mountains, Simone's passion is flying helicopters. He owns an Écureuil AS350 B3 helicopter, which he keeps in Nepal. AS350 helicopters are so powerful that in 2005 a French pilot, Didier Delsalle, managed to touch the top of Mount Everest with one. Even though the Écureil is very light and made to fly at high altitudes, it had to be upgraded for that particular flight, as helicopters are usually not supposed to go that high. The air resistance is insufficient for the rotors to operate fully. There used to be a lot of Russian MI-8 helicopters in Nepal, but most of them were flown until they crashed. Simone's helicopter was transported from Italy to Nepal in a cargo plane and is now used almost daily for taking supplies to Everest Base Camp. The regulations of his Italian insurance company allow only European pilots to fly his helicopter, so Simone flies it as often as his time allows. He used to operate his charter service for Fishtail Air, a Nepali company.

As the weather forecast was pretty bad for the next few days, Simone, Jon, and I went to Namche Bazaar in Simone's helicopter, which was empty after Simone had flown some supplies from Lukla to Base Camp. We certainly would not miss anything on the mountain in this weather, our bodies would have time to recover at the lower altitude, and it would take only a day's trekking to get back to Base Camp. In Namche Bazaar, which lies at less than 4000 meters, I could sleep well again. The following morning we went for a run and crossed over to the next valley, Thame.

After three days in Namche Bazaar, we had yet another chance to grab a ride in Simone's helicopter, and so we flew back to Base Camp. The weather had improved enough for us to go on our next acclimatization rotation, which we intended to do on the normal route rather than on our planned ascent route. The sole reason for this was the fact that we wanted to achieve our goal in alpine style and did not want to spoil the novelty of the climb by too many reconnaissance trips. On April 26 Simone, Jon, and I ascended to Camp 2, where we spent a pleasurable evening. Our spirits were high, we were having fun and filled with positive energy. I was convinced that the three of us were acclimatized well enough to spend two nights at Camp 4 on the South Col at 8000 meters. After this acclimatization rotation, we would be ready for the big traverse! I wanted to get acclimatized as quickly as possible in order to use the weather window in May. Since we were climbing without supplemental oxygen, we needed twice as much time to adapt to the altitude. Those who climb Everest with bottled oxygen only need one night at Camp 3 at 7300 meters to be ready for the summit. For climbers with oxygen, the summit of Everest (8848 meters) is effectively reduced to what they would experience at 6500–7000 meters without it. We, on the other hand, needed to spend at least two nights at Camp 3 and at least one night at Camp 4 at 8000 meters to avoid getting altitude illness during the summit attempt. We were pressed for time and wanted to use every possible day on the mountain to acclimatize.

At the crack of dawn the following morning, a group of Sherpas was moving toward the Lhotse Face. They were "fixing" the mountain—affixing ropes that would help the clients of commercial expeditions reach the higher camps more easily and safely. They were also under pressure to finish this work in time. It is a tough job; carrying heavy equipment to 7000 meters and attaching the ropes to the mountain requires a lot of strength. The previous day had been a bit disappointing for the Sherpas. Working with three Western guides, they had encountered a crevasse they couldn't get around just below Camp 3, necessitating removal of all the gear in order to start from scratch on a different route.

The Sherpas' rope-fixing and our climbing coincided on the Lhotse Face, which has a gradient of between 30 and 50 degrees. This is not too steep: one can usually walk up it, using axes only where there is bare ice. The previous day we had noticed that there was still a lot of snow on the left side of the face, which would make our ascent pretty easy. It was only 800 meters to Camp 3, where the Russian Alexey Bolotov and Kazakh Denis Urubko had left their tent for us. The pair wanted to open a new route on the Southwest Face of Everest. We shared our base camp and supported each other as much as we could, alternately using the same tent and sharing other equipment on the mountain. The two had descended from Camp 3 the day before. If our physical condition allowed it, we wanted to set up camp on the South Col after having spent two or three nights at Camp 3.

We took our time and waited for the weather to warm before we set out from Camp 2. Just below the Lhotse Face we met an American mountain guide who told us not to use the fixed ropes. I assured him that we would stay away from them and would not disturb the Sherpas doing their work. We all had two ice axes, which meant that we did not rely on the fixed ropes.

After I had climbed over the bergschrund, I immediately traversed 50 meters diagonally to the left. One reason was to keep a safe distance from the ropes and not to get in the way of the Sherpas doing their work. The other reason was not to get hit by falling ice: higher up on the mountain, two Sherpas were hacking out a platform, sending chunks of ice in our direction. I waited for Jon, and then, as Simone was still behind, we used the time to take pictures. It is always good to do this during waiting periods rather than losing too much time taking pictures during climbing. And taking photos with Jon is easy: he is fit, and he is able to move on the mountain independently.

Finally Simone arrived, and we continued. After about an hour we reached the level of the tent, but getting there required traversing to the right and stepping over the fixed ropes. In order to make it easier for everyone, we looked for a section that was snowy rather than icy. A couple of meters above us were two Sherpas, who were attached to an ice screw and belaying the leader of the team, Mingma Tenzing from Phortse in the Everest region. Mingma Tenzing was quite a way above them and climbing up ice.

Jon was the first to traverse to the right underneath the Sherpas' belay point. He had barely moved when the Sherpas started shouting at him. I reached the same point about a minute after Jon. There was tension in the thin air. Jon continued to the tent, and I saw that Mingma was rappelling straight toward me. I stopped him with one hand, as I was not secured to anything and wanted to avoid tumbling down the mountain. "Why are you touching me?" he shouted. I said that there were 500 meters below us and that I was not attached to a rope. "Why are you here?" he raged. "Because our tent is over there." I explained to him that we had made an effort to ascend on the left-hand side in the snow to avoid getting in their way. "You do your job, and we do ours. There is enough space for all of us."

Trying to ease the tension, I offered to help them fix the ropes as soon as I had dumped my gear in our tent. But this seemed to make him even more furious. When Simone came into the vicinity, Mingma started to swing both his ice axes toward him.

"What are you doing?" Simone screamed. Panicking, he lost his temper, and to make matters worse added the Nepali word *machikne*, which equates to "motherfucker" and is a severe insult to a Nepali.

The situation escalated from there. Simone and Mingma had a heated debate, during which Mingma threatened Simone with his ice axe several times. I was convinced that it would have been better to shut up. But then, I am a person inclined to keep quiet rather than add fuel to the fire. I shrugged my shoulders and wondered why Mingma was so upset. What was his problem? At that moment, I neither knew what *machikne* meant, nor did I have an inkling where this exchange of harsh words would lead.

I let Simone and Mingma continue their discussion and joined Jon in the tent. A little later we noticed that all the Sherpas had stopped working and were rappelling down to Camp 3. At first I assumed that they had been working hard since early morning and our arrival was a welcome reason for them to call it a day. It was not late, but a fierce wind had been blowing for an hour. However, the fact that the rope-fixing had stopped made me feel uncomfortable. The Sherpas' hard work had probably taken a toll, and it is known that too much stress leads to overreaction. I was worried that the expedition operators would be furious and blame us for their clients not being able to reach Camp 3 on schedule. As I felt somehow responsible and wanted to improve the situation, I took the remaining 260 meters of rope and fixed the rest of the route to Camp 3. What I had not thought about was the Sherpas' dignity. I had not considered that I would hurt their pride by taking over their work and doing it so quickly. I was simply not aware that this would mean a severe loss of face for them. My thinking, which in hindsight seems naïve, was that even though Jon, Simone, and I did not need the fixed ropes, we could help the Sherpas and work together with them instead of being at odds.

While I was fixing the last bit of rope on the upper section, Simone was in constant radio contact with Camp 2. I could not hear what they were talking about. In any case, Simone decided that it would be better not to spend the night at Camp 3 but to instead descend to Camp 2 and resolve the situation. I was a bit annoyed, as we had planned to acclimatize for two nights at Camp 3 and then continue up to the South Col and set up our tent there. Now we were going down instead.

We reached Camp 2 just before dark. There, the American mountain guide Melissa Arnot warned us that the Sherpas were infuriated with us for having climbed on the Lhotse Face. Apparently she had been on the radio all afternoon in an effort to calm the situation. We all sat in the relatively big gear tent and discussed the events of the day. Shortly after Melissa went back to her tent, she came running back, shouting that we should try to get away as quickly as possible because the Sherpas had formed a mob.

I expected a heavy discussion. I assumed that we would talk about who was right and who was wrong. I was ready to apologize for having been up there, even though I thought no one had the right to deny others access to the mountain.

Then we stepped out of our tent.

Hooded figures with rocks in their hands were approaching us. Simone and Jon ran away. When the Sherpas marched toward our tent, Marty Schmidt, a New Zealand mountain guide who happened to be there, walked up to one of them and tried to knock the rock out of his hand. They kicked and punched Marty, he was hit by a rock, and someone whacked him in the face. He defended himself and struck back.

Mingma, the leader of the mob, came up to me, and before I was even able to utter a word, he punched my nose. Just like that.

The next thing I knew, a big rock hit my face.

I was dumbfounded and could not quite comprehend what was happening. I crouched down on my knees and put my hands over my head. Otherwise I did not even try to defend myself; if I had done so, they would all have attacked me. Another Sherpa, standing above me, was aiming a brick-sized rock at my head when Melissa got between us. Attacking a woman would have been against the Sherpas' mores.

I grabbed the opportunity and dashed back into the tent, but I came out again after a big rock was thrown into the tent and missed me by a whisker. When I saw Jon and Simone, who were standing a distance from the tent, I walked up to them and said: "I think the expedition is over."

At that moment the mob moved toward us again and assaulted Jon. Another Western mountain guide came to our aid and made the Sherpas back off. Jon and Simone made a break for the glacier, but I was stopped. I returned to the tent with Marty, who had a gash on his head.

"Give him to us! We will kill him!" About one hundred belligerent men had gathered in front of the tent, calling for me.

Greg Vernovage, another American mountain guide, and Melissa guarded the tent and tried to keep the Sherpas at bay. A lone Sherpa, Pang Nuru, was standing next to them. He had nothing to do with us but was obviously perturbed by the situation and knew that this was just not right.

I could hear a fierce discussion. The Sherpas ordered me to come out. I would be the first they would beat to death, and when they had finished with me they would go for the other two.

I felt powerless and could not see a way out. How could we possibly turn the situation in our favor? What would happen to us? It was over. I couldn't do anything. My hands were tied.

I thought about how ridiculous the situation was. How many expeditions had I been on and come back from in one piece? How many critical situations had I survived? And now I was crouching in a tent on Mount Everest, just about to be killed by a mob of Sherpas. This was impossible. The whole situation so absurd that I had no hope. The Sherpas were unpredictable, but I would probably not survive. I started to imagine how my life would end by stoning.

After a while the Sherpas ordered Simone, who had insulted Mingma, to come out. This gave me reason to believe we might have a chance. Simone, who was hiding somewhere on the glacier, returned and was pushed inside the tent. Some time later, Melissa came in and told Simone what the Sherpas demanded: They wanted him to get down on his knees and apologize for the insulting words he had uttered on the Lhotse Face. When Simone stepped out of the tent, the Sherpas went for him immediately. He knelt down and apologized, and the Sherpas kicked him in the face.

In the middle of this commotion, we were suddenly accused of having been on the Lhotse Face without a climbing permit, which was ridiculous. After Base Camp confirmed that we did have a permit, the Sherpas started to withdraw but told Melissa and Greg that if we were not gone within one hour, they would kill us.

When Melissa finally informed us that they had all gone, we hastily packed our gear, wanting to get away as quickly as possible. Since our tent was in the upper section of Camp 2, we left from the back to avoid having to walk past all the other tents. The best way for us to sneak away quietly was through the crevasses, but we were scared that the Sherpas would follow us. I remembered a ladder over a huge crevasse lower down the mountain. My goal was to cross this crevasse and then remove the ladder, which would stop anyone from following us. At that point I would not have put anything past them, but nobody came.

We still did not have a clue what to expect at Camp 1. Maybe the Sherpas had radioed their peers and we would be greeted with the same vengeance we had encountered at Camp 2. We were very apprehensive when we reached the first tents, but the climbers and Sherpas seemed pretty relaxed. They asked us what had happened and shook their heads in disbelief. We were very brief with our answers, eager as we were to continue down. What else would come our way?

As we neared the Khumbu Icefall, it began to get dark. We were worried that the Sherpas had told others at Base Camp to wait for us in the icefall and assault us under cover of night. I could not begin to imagine what it would be like to be attacked while crossing a crevasse on a ladder. Even though an ice axe is usually not needed in the icefall, I was firmly holding mine in my hand, just in case. Fortunately we got safely through the icefall. After we reached our tent at Base Camp we went to sleep wearing our helmets and holding our ice axes.

Jon and Simone remained at Base Camp, but I wanted to get away as quickly as possible. Simone organized his helicopter, which took me to Lukla the following day. I'd had enough. However, two days later Jon and Simone called me back, saying that some sort of "peace talk" had been planned at Base Camp. We all signed a handwritten agreement that stated that we forgave each other and that we would not resort to violence in the future.

In the meantime, Tenji and some other Sherpas had collected our gear from Camp 2, and I was amazed to see that nothing was missing. As one more night at Base Camp was enough for me, I took a helicopter to Lukla and then to Kathmandu the next morning to grab the next possible flight back to Switzerland. I just wanted to go home. I was seriously fed up with Nepal, at least for the time being.

▲ ▲ ▲

I was on my way back to Switzerland when my friend Alexey Bolotov fell to his death between Base Camp and Camp 1. He was climbing on an alternative route to avoid the Khumbu Icefall when his rope broke as he was rappelling. He was considered one of the best mountaineers in the world and was only fifty years old. I remember patting him on the shoulder, as he seemed pretty upset when I left Base Camp after the Sherpas' assault. I recall telling him: "You are my role model. If I want to, I have at least another thirteen years of climbing the highest peaks."

Alexey will always have a special place in my heart. He was my idol. After the attacks he kept on repeating the same words during every meeting. After we had discussed the events for the umpteenth time, he got up and said in his Russian-accented English: "This is bullshit!" Then he stepped out of the tent.

Expeditions frequently do not go as planned. In the run-up to the expedition, I dealt with all eventualities and imagined all the things that could go wrong. What would the conditions on the mountain have to be like in order to complete the traverse from Everest to Lhotse? I had carefully worked out how we would have to acclimatize in order to stay fit and strong above 8000 meters for such a long time. We would have to spend at least two nights at 8000 meters, which would cost us a lot of strength and energy. And before we could be ready for the summit attempt, we would have to recover and descend to the valley at below 4000 meters for five to seven days. On top of that we would have to be extremely careful during our acclimatization rotations. If you get sick once, the expedition is likely to be over for you. A common cold often means the end. When spending so much time above 8000 meters, even the slightest cough can have a detrimental effect on your performance and force you to abandon an expedition.

There were many factors that could affect the success of such an undertaking. But I was convinced that we had prepared for almost everything and that all of us were physically fit enough to take on the challenge. Then our project took an unexpected turn, and it was no longer about mountaineering. All of a sudden we were involved in a clash between cultures, a clash that was about power and money.

Most Western mountaineers go climbing because of their enthusiasm and motivation for the sport. For the Sherpas in the Himalaya, mountaineering is one of the few opportunities to make money and earn a living. Why should Sherpas care about who climbs Everest with or without the use of supplemental oxygen? Their job is to get as many clients to the top of the world as possible. They make their money working for commercial expeditions and get hardly anything from independent mountaineers like me. Yet, after all, it is their summit—their Mount Everest. And the culture and background of the Nepali people is very different from our culture, which inevitably leads to tensions in the long run.

At the same time, the Sherpas are in a tricky situation. They fill the role of mountain guides but have no authority. As opposed to European guides, they are at the end of the decision-making chain. If Matterhorn guides tell their clients that they have to turn back due to lack of experience, they will turn back. On Everest it is otherwise. It often happens that clients do not listen or they disregard the Sherpas' advice and opinions.

I witnessed this when I climbed Everest in 2012. The Nepali-born Canadian Shriya Shah-Klorfine reached the summit at 2:00 p.m., which was far too late. It had taken her seventeen hours from the South Col to the top, and, even though her Sherpas told her to turn back several times, she continued. She said it had been her dream to reach the top of the world, and she had paid a lot of money for it. And then the inevitable happened: she ran out of oxygen on the descent and took her last breath just below the Hillary Step. The Sherpas continued down without her. It must be frustrating for them to be ignored and not respected most of the time.

In my opinion the brawl at Camp 2 was nothing more than a demonstration of power. The Sherpas are not stupid and know how much money is generated on their mountain. Nepal makes exorbitant amounts of money from climbing permits, but most of it ends up in the deep pockets of the government officials. The big commercial operators live abroad and employ their own mountain guides. The Sherpas have to do the hard work of load carrying, and, as is so often the case elsewhere, those who work most are not necessarily those who earn most. It is obvious that the Sherpas want a bigger piece of the pie.

A similar power struggle happened the following year. After sixteen Sherpas were tragically killed in an avalanche in April 2014, the Sherpa community was split into two groups. One group was willing to continue to work on the mountain, while the other group argued that it would be disrespectful to the dead. But at the end of the day, it was a matter of putting the government under pressure to improve the insurance system for the Sherpa families. Both were valid arguments, but the fact that the second group threatened the first group and denied them access to the mountain was incomprehensible. Due to the ensuing strike, the climbing season ended early that spring.

▲ ▲ ▲

I guess that when the first rock flew through Camp 2 on that fateful day, it released a lot of tension from people who had felt humiliated for a while. There were various reasons why the three of us fell victim to this situation. We had certainly been at the wrong place at the wrong time. Simone's angry words on the Lhotse Face sparked the situation, and the fact that I had finished the Sherpas' rope-fixing did not help either. Even though it was well intended, I now know that it actually exacerbated the situation.

An additional factor is that some people do not like that Jon, Simone, and I move with such speed and persistence on the mountain.

The events on Everest in 2013 triggered a lot of comments, and everyone interpreted the situation differently. The facts got mixed up, and in the end nobody really knew who said what, who touched whom, and who kicked off the falling ice. There was also confusion about an alleged climbing ban on that day. Apparently the commercial operators had agreed not to let anybody but the Sherpas climb on the Lhotse Face that day, but I had not heard anything about this agreement.

However, all these discussions seem irrelevant in the light of what happened at Camp 2 that day. I was shocked by how aggressive and belligerent some of the Sherpas were. Up to that day I could have never imagined that a Sherpa would be so violent. I can deal with arguments, but in this case I had misinterpreted the strong emotions of the Sherpas. I had not considered that things worked differently in Nepal than in Europe, that a different culture would solve conflicts differently, and that other power structures applied. I was not sensitive enough to sufficiently consider all the cultural differences.

I had actually been pretty lucky. The situation could have easily gotten worse. Had Melissa Arnot not inserted herself between the Sherpas and me, I would probably have died. I am very grateful to everyone who helped me in this situation, including Marty Schmidt, who was killed in an avalanche on K2 later that year. Melissa and Marty were among the few people who did not put their heads in the sand, thinking the problem was none of their business.

The immense fear of dying I had on that day changed my perception of Nepal. Rationally, I knew that we had not been the cause but the trigger for the conflict. I knew that nobody wanted to kill me just because I was Ueli Steck, and I also knew pretty soon after I had returned to Switzerland that I would return to Nepal one day. The mountains were a very important part of my life, and I would never give up mountaineering. Nepal is home to the highest mountains in the world. Climbing higher than 8000 meters remained a challenge that fascinated me.

Of course, I was free to choose which mountains I would climb in the future. I did not necessarily have to go back to such a commercialized mountain as Mount Everest has become. Due to the infrastructure and the support of supplemental oxygen, the highest mountain in the world has become one of the easiest 8000-meter peaks. Authorities in Nepal are considering installing a ladder on the Hillary Step, which is the bottleneck on the south side. This would enable more people to reach the summit. The development on Mount Everest cannot be stopped or reversed. It will remain the highest mountain in the world. It will continue to attract many people. Nepal and local operators will continue to use it to make money.

The dark shadow those events had cast on Mount Everest would stay with me for a while. It made me feel sad, though, to have lost the magic of this mountain. I consciously made an effort to recall reaching the summit with Tenji in 2012. It was a warm and calm day. As equal partners—not as "Sherpa" and "client"—we climbed together with other Sherpas, who were fixing the rope to the summit. I wanted to preserve the memory of Tenji and me standing happily on the highest point on Earth, not the image of the violent mob at Camp 2.

However, coming to terms with my emotions was difficult. At the moment when I had realized that the Sherpas wanted to kill me, my whole world had split apart. Even though I had not considered them friends, I had shared a cup of coffee with some of them—and suddenly they had wanted to break my skull with rocks. I was shocked, and it had changed my view of the world.

I had long been prepared for the unexpected to happen on a mountain. I had lost too many friends and colleagues on climbs, and I knew that it could happen to me any time. Even though you never really expect it, it is the reality of alpinism. Sometimes people do not come home. I had always been aware that my life could be over in an instant, that there was no guarantee. I had accepted the risks of mountaineering. What I struggled with was people's behavior and the aggression I had encountered.

I had generally had a positive attitude and believed in the good in people, but all of a sudden I had lost faith in humanity. I realized that I might have relied on the wrong people, no matter which country they were from. I found it hard to trust those around me, no matter whether they were mountaineering colleagues, business partners, or even friends. I looked at them differently, in a more critical way.

I started to withdraw. I switched off my cell phone, bought a prepaid SIM card, and only shared the number with my family and closest friends. I did not want to be in touch with the rest of the world. Hordes of journalists came to my house trying to get an interview, but I refused. I had given my statement on the events on Everest, and I was not willing to say more. Even Nicole, my wife, found it hard to get through to me. Of course, we talked about what had happened on Everest, but this was only right after I got home and then only briefly. I avoided telling her the details as I did not want her to worry even more the next time I was on an expedition. On top of that I thought it would be pointless trying to describe how I had felt up there. Only someone who had been through that experience could really understand, someone who had faced death. It was not easy for Nicole, who wanted to help and support me, but I needed to find my own way of getting over it.

My cure was climbing. Before my departure for Everest I had already planned another expedition for 2013. After two failed attempts on the South Face of Annapurna I, I finally felt ready to go back there. The expedition would start in September and was a welcome distraction. It became my goal, and I started training like a maniac.

It was still May when Jon Griffith and I hooked up to do one of my favorite training routes, climbing the Mönch in the Swiss Alps all the way from the valley. The route starts in Grindelwald Grund, goes up to the Kleine Scheidegg, and then continues via the Nollen to the summit: 18 kilometers of distance and 3100 meters of elevation gain. I was breaking trail, which was strenuous in the deep snow, but it helped me switch off. I was living for the moment and enjoyed it despite the immense effort. The descent was quick: we took only forty minutes to get from the top to the Jungfraujoch railway station. We stopped there and had a well-deserved cup of coffee at the bar. It felt good to be back on my old stomping grounds.

I did a lot of running over the summer. One of my favorite routes went from the Stechelberg mountain up the Sefinen Valley, then down via the Sefinafurgga and back up to the Blüemlisalp Hut, where I usually treated myself to a cheese sandwich and continued on to the village of Kandersteg. What I really like about trail running is that it simply requires a pair of running shoes and a backpack containing something to drink and eat. My ambitious training plan gave my life some structure again. I looked ahead, and all I could see was Annapurna and the incessant training for it.

Since I had not worn myself out on my spring expedition in Nepal, I did not need a recovery phase and was able to complete some very long and intense training sessions. These gave me the feeling of being my own master again. On Everest things had been out of my control, and I had been at the mercy of others. I had been used to making my own decisions and acting autonomously, when suddenly I was confronted with an enraged mob armed with rocks. There was nothing I could do. I never wanted to feel so powerless again, and in order to forget Everest I threw myself into my training for Annapurna. I did not realize then that I was only pushing away past events and not really dealing with them.

ANNAPURNA I
FIRST THE GLORY, THEN THE FALL FROM GRACE

The highest summit of the Annapurna range, Annapurna I, had been on my mind for more than ten years. It was Swiss climber Erhard Loretan who kindled my fascination with its South Face. In my very early climbing days in the Himalaya, I had attempted the North Face of Jannu twice, in 2002 and 2003. Neither attempt of this 7000-meter peak in eastern Nepal was successful, but Erhard Loretan's presence made both trips very special. In 1995 he had become the third person to climb all fourteen 8000-meter peaks, and he had been one of my heroes, someone I looked up to with respect. I was in my mid-twenties, with very little high-altitude experience, and I was lucky to benefit from the knowledge of this old-timer in his early forties. During the long waiting periods for better weather, I absorbed Erhard's tales about the "good old days."

One of the mountains that kept coming up in his stories was Annapurna. Together with Swiss mountaineer Norbert Joos, known as Noppa, he traversed all three peaks of the Annapurna range in alpine style, which was an extraordinary achievement. At the time Annapurna had been Erhard's sixth and Norbert's third 8000-meter peak. No matter how different the two men seemed at first glance—Erhard was rather introverted, while Noppa was more of an extrovert—they seemed to complement each other perfectly. After they had reached the east summit via the east ridge and spent the night in a snow cave, they traversed to the central summit the following day. In order to reach the saddle between the central and the main summit, which is to the west, they had to rappel down a rock face for about 100 meters. During their rappel, they found that the face was unclimbable and that it would thus be impossible to climb back up and descend via the east ridge. They continued and reached the 8091-meter main summit of Annapurna on October 24, 1984, at 2:30 p.m., becoming the twelfth expedition to reach the top of Annapurna.

Now the real adventure began: descending the wildly fissured and avalanche-prone north ridge. A postcard indicating this normal descent route was the only reference they had. In later years Erhard wrote about the difficulties of finding the route: "In fact, it's all about taking the right turn in the small zone that separates life from death. I guess this is the whole definition of survival." For two and a half days they wandered about heavily crevassed terrain interspersed with vertical rock walls and overhanging ice cliffs, which they rappelled. When the terrain finally flattened, they were far from safe. Avalanches and falling seracs posed the next threat. They almost got caught in an avalanche but were lucky and only got dusted with about 5 centimeters of snow. Erhard told me that during the entire descent there were always three of them: Noppa, himself, and fear.

The two had chosen the Dutch route, the shortest route on the north side. Despite its threat of serac fall and avalanche, the French route, which leads across wide glaciers a little bit farther to the west, is still considered the easiest ascent route on Annapurna. In 1950 this was the route of the first ascent, which made Annapurna the first 8000-meter peak to be scaled. Back then France's best alpinists traveled to Nepal to overcome the "death zone" above 7000 meters and "conquer" an 8000-meter peak. Today we know that at an altitude of 7000 meters or higher, the oxygen saturation of the hemoglobin in arterial blood drops to such a low level that even a perfectly acclimatized body can no longer recuperate. Inevitably the body gets so depleted that it is no longer possible to stay up high. You would die of altitude illness.

At a time when alpinism was still about the conquest of mountains, the first ascent of Annapurna, under the leadership of Maurice Herzog, embraced the myths of heroic deeds and nationalism. Nepal had only just opened its borders to foreigners. The available maps had turned out to be so inaccurate that the French had no choice but to reconnoiter the area in the spring of 1950. Annapurna was not even their initial objective. They had set their eyes on doing the first ascent of Dhaulagiri I. They changed their minds when they saw that its east face as well as its north face, which they had only reached after a very long approach march, were probably hopeless. Hence, the expedition set up its base camp on Annapurna in the middle of May.

They first tried their luck on the north ridge but had to abandon their attempt due to too much difficulty. They then turned to the north face, where they set up five consecutive high camps. After a stormy night Maurice Herzog and Louis Lachenal started out from the last camp at 7300 meters on June 3, 1950. Against all odds, they fought their way up and reached the summit of Annapurna in the afternoon. They were the first humans to reach the summit of an 8000-meter peak.

The descent turned out to be epic, though, and dampened their euphoria about their success. Herzog and Lachenal were so exhausted that they probably would not have survived had it not been for Gaston Rébuffat and Lionel Terray, who came to their rescue. After the four climbers spent one night at the highest camp, they were unable to find Camp 4 in a raging storm and were forced to spend a night in a crevasse in the bitter cold. The following day they continued struggling on the descent and barely survived an avalanche that came thundering down on them. After six days the four finally reached the safety of their base camp. Lachenal and Herzog had suffered such severe frostbite that the expedition doctor performed amputations along the jungle trail back to Kathmandu. In the end Herzog lost all his fingers and toes, Lachenal all his toes and parts of his feet. Both had to pay a very high price for their first ascent of an 8000-meter peak.

Back in France huge controversies emerged about what had happened on the mountain. Herzog was in charge of the official expedition report and failed to include his companions' statements, which were only made public in the 1990s, just after Lachenal's original manuscript was released. As was common with climbers in the 1950s, the French team had taken epinephrine and amphetamines. How much these influenced the climbers' decisions is impossible to say, but they would have certainly helped them to extend their limits.

The high avalanche danger on the normal route as well as the fact that all the other routes are extremely technical is probably the reason why Annapurna is the least climbed 8000-meter peak. With a mortality rate of 30 percent, it is considered even more dangerous than K2 in Pakistan. Through the spring of 2016, 244 people had reached the summit and 71 had died trying. (For comparison, Everest, with 7655 ascents and 284 fatalities, has a mortality rate of 3.7 percent.)

▲▲▲

Erhard Loretan was convinced that the biggest challenge on Annapurna was its South Face. It was first climbed in 1970 and was the second route to the top, which had not been reached in twenty years. In 1964 Shishapangma became the last 8000-meter peak to be climbed, accomplished by a team of Chinese mountaineers. This meant that new and greater challenges from now on would not be simply peaks but previously unclimbed and more difficult routes. Only a small group of climbing freaks was interested in tackling new 6000-meter and 7000-meter peaks.

One of these challenges was the 2500-meter Annapurna South Face—one of the highest and steepest rock faces in the Himalaya. A British expedition under the leadership of Sir Chris Bonington was brave enough to attempt it in the spring of 1970. Bonington not only gathered a team of the twelve strongest climbers, he also managed to get these individualists, all extremely eager to reach the summit, to work as a team to reach their goal. The team chose a route on the left of the face, which elegantly circumnavigated the central rock bastion. They fixed 4500 meters of rope to negotiate the difficult sections, used supplemental oxygen, and set up six permanent high camps. Given the logistics of such an undertaking, carrying the loads became a decisive factor for their success. Getting the necessary gear up the mountain was more energy-sapping than getting the team to advance on the route.

Bonington later recalled that deciding who should do what on this expedition and keeping every single team member motivated at the same time had been the most difficult task of his life. After Tom Frost and Mick Burke had worn themselves out struggling to climb the wall for four long weeks, and Martin Boysen and Nick Estcourt were exhausted from carrying loads up the mountain, he replaced the four climbers with Don Whillans and Dougal Haston. The two were still relatively fresh, and with the groundwork of their colleagues they were able to set up a last high camp and attempt the summit. They were running out of time, as storms had already started to flare up and the monsoon season was just around the corner. It was Bonington himself who supplied the summit team with food and propane before the two climbers left their camp on the morning of May 27.

Haston and Whillans had planned to pitch a seventh camp above the rock band, but around midday they decided to dump their gear and go straight for the summit. Without the weight of their backpacks, they made good progress. After they had negotiated the short summit wall via a ramp from right to left, they suddenly found themselves on the summit ridge, where Whillans fixed the rope to a bolt. A snowstorm was already raging in the south, while the weather was still beautiful in the north. The terrain was flat, and they easily reached the top via a snowy crest. Three days later Mick Burke and Tom Frost started another summit attempt, but they failed, and the fast-approaching monsoon ended the expedition.

This magnificent success, which was based on joint efforts, marked the beginning of a new period of high-altitude mountaineering, which was all about climbing the biggest faces in the world. Due to technical difficulties, the oxygen-deprived air, and in particular the great efforts that were needed for such an undertaking, the risks of such expeditions increased exponentially. The expedition to the South Face of Annapurna was also an example of the close relationship between joy and sorrow. Even though Bonington's team was unscathed during the ascent, Ian Clough and Mike Thompson were hit by an ice avalanche on their descent between Camp 2 and Camp 1, and a huge block of ice buried Clough forever.

Fourteen years later the South Face of Annapurna was yet again the scene for a milestone in alpinism. In October 1984, two Spaniards, Nil Bohigas and Enric Lucas, opened a new line to the central summit (8051 meters). They climbed alpine style, which meant that they did not use any external help, supplemental oxygen, or fixed ropes. I was particularly impressed by Lucas, who now leads a withdrawn life somewhere in the Pyrenees. He knew what he wanted and had always followed his own path. Bohigas and Lucas climbed the route for themselves. It was their own personal adventure, and they climbed it out of passion and conviction. When they came back Lucas avoided any hype surrounding him. He now leads a simple life, enjoys going for runs, and just wants to be left in peace. He does not give interviews, which is the reason why there is very little information about this expedition.

Eight years after the ascent of Bohigas and Lucas, Frenchmen Pierre Béghin and Jean-Christophe Lafaille tried their luck on the South Face. They intended to take the direct line to the main summit of Annapurna. The route led straight up the center of the face, which the Brits had climbed on the left and the Spaniards on the right. In his tales Erhard Loretan described their undertaking with so much enthusiasm and passion that I was completely hooked.

The pair left their advanced base camp on October 7, 1992, and ascended to their first bivouac at the so-called Pear at 6500 meters. The following morning they moved up the rope they had fixed the previous day to help them get across the first steep section in the middle of the face. From here it was flatter, and they had no problems in reaching the base of the headwall, the rocky section on the upper third of the face. At 6900 meters they hacked a platform into the ice, set up their second bivouac, and spent two nights there. The rocky bulwark of the headwall towered above them, with an abyss of 1600 meters below.

They started out from their bivouac at about 4:00 a.m. Pierre had expected to climb the gully on the face, but they had to move to the left and could not climb the big dihedral as they had intended. As the weather was deteriorating, they were forced to set up a bivouac in a pretty much unprotected space at about 7400 meters. Pitching a tent turned out to be impossible, so they crouched on a ledge for the whole night and following morning until the weather finally cleared. Neither of them was willing to give up. Hoping they had sat out the bad weather, they continued their ascent.

But when the next storm pounded them at 7500 meters, they had no other choice but to retreat. Descending the steep rock face demanded quite a few rappels, during which they had to leave some gear behind. Because Béghin, who was the older and more experienced of the pair, wanted to save equipment, he instructed Lafaille, who had just placed a peg, to remove it again. He was convinced that the Friend he had put into a crack would suffice as the sole fixing point. But when Béghin put his weight on the rope, he pulled the bolt out of the crack. Without being able to help, Lafaille had to watch his friend tumble down into the abyss.

Stranded and alone in the midst of this gigantic face, Lafaille was now fighting for his life. Béghin had taken the rope and his backpack, which held most of their equipment, down into the void with him. Lafaille took a while to recover from his shock before he was able to continue his descent. Without a rope he had no choice but to climb down the steep sections. On the ledge where the pair had bivouacked forty-eight hours earlier, he found a 20-meter length of 6-millimeter rope as well as some food. The raging storm forced him to remain there for thirty hours, alone with his thoughts about Pierre.

On the morning of October 12 the wind finally abated. Without any safety gear, Lafaille knocked tent pegs into the ice, threaded rope through, and rappelled off them. With a 20-meter climbing rope, this was an endless undertaking and was aggravated by the fact that Lafaille had lost one of his crampons. He was on his last legs when he reached the fixed rope just above their first camp. After he had managed to clip into the rope and rappel down, falling rocks hit him about 150 meters above the camp. Unconscious, he slid down the rope all the way to the camp, where he came to. Still dangling on the rope, he found that his right arm was broken. Unable to pitch the tent, he wrapped himself in it and passed the night. He was close to giving up.

Lafaille stayed the whole of the following day at Camp 1 and was only able to get back on his feet and continue down in the evening. Weakened and traumatized by the events and his injuries, it took him all night to reach the bergschrund, not arriving until 8:00 a.m. With nearly the last ounce of his strength, he crawled to the camp of the Slovenian team but was devastated to find it deserted. Once again he had to pull himself together and find the strength and will-power to continue to his own camp. On his way down, the liaison officer of his expedition came toward him. Finally he was safe!

I could not stop thinking about the dramatic story of Béghin and Lafaille. The fact that these two top-class mountaineers were forced back on the South Face of Annapurna meant that it must be really difficult. When in 2005 a German translation of Lafaille's 2003 *Prisonnier de l'Annapurna* was published, I was captivated reading about the 1992 expedition as well as his successful ascent in 2002, when he climbed the face via the east ridge with Alberto Iñurrategi. Finally I had to admit to myself that the project of the two Frenchmen fascinated me so much that I wanted to finish their route on the South Face of Annapurna. Their chosen line had the advantage of being objectively pretty safe, as it was not threatened by cornice or serac fall. However, it had the disadvantage of being exposed to the sun for many hours of the day. While this made climbing more pleasant, it also made the route more prone to avalanches and rockfall due to the huge temperature differences between day and night.

In the autumn of 2006 I finally traveled to Nepal to have a look at the face. It was impressively steep. I realized that I had to be extremely quick if I wanted to climb it during a period of clement weather and be back at its base in good time. The only way to climb the face quickly would be to climb light, taking the minimal amount of gear. I began formulating a plan for a solo attempt. If I could master all of the technical difficulties without making a mistake, and if I were to be at my very best physically, I might be able to pull it off.

The following spring I attempted the South Face for the first time. In preparation for the expedition I trained a lot for endurance and practiced climbing without a rope. In order to be well acclimatized I spent many weeks in the vicinity of Everest in Nepal. Nicole and I climbed Cholatse, a 6000-meter peak in the region. After our expedition Nicole went home, and I soloed the west face of Pumori (7161 meters) in twenty-four hours. I also spent many hours running at an altitude of 4000–5000 meters in the Khumbu. I felt fit and prepared.

Putting together and finding funds for the Annapurna expedition was not easy, but once it was done I felt comfortable and happy with the team. The photographer Robert Bösch, also known as Röbi, came with me to document the ascent. Bruno Roth and Jacqueline Schwerzmann were going to film the events on Annapurna for Swiss television. Michael Wulzinger, editor of the German magazine *Der Spiegel*, and Oswald Oelz, who came as the expedition doctor, were also part of the team. After a few frustrating weeks waiting for better weather, the skies cleared, and I could finally leave base camp. As the way to the bergschrund was heavily crevassed, Röbi accompanied me to the bottom of the face for safety reasons. When he turned back, I started to climb. Suddenly my mind went black. I cannot remember what happened. The next thing I knew I was coming to with my face buried in the snow. I tried to make sense of it. I must have climbed for about 200 to 300 meters when I was struck by a rock and fell. My climbing helmet was broken. I had been extremely lucky that I had escaped relatively unscathed: concussion, bruises, and a few muscle strains.

Even though this expedition was over pretty abruptly, and I'd had a brush with death, I immediately started to plan my next attempt for the following year. This time I wanted to climb the South Face in a roped party with Simon Anthamatten, an experienced Swiss ice climber. In the spring of 2008 we acclimatized on Tengkangpoche, where we opened a new route on the North Face, an achievement for which we each received the acclaimed Piolet d'Or, the highest award in alpinism.

Although our trip had started so well, our winning streak did not continue. First we had to wait two weeks for the weather to clear and allow us to set foot onto the wall. We then climbed up to 6000 meters, but so much snow had been dumped on the route that avalanches came thundering past us even before the sun touched the face. We were forced to descend—conditions were far too dangerous—but we did not give up hope and decided to wait for the weather to improve and the snow to melt.

But then the expedition took another turn. My satellite phone rang, and we received a call for help: an expedition on the east ridge had run into trouble. Accomplished Spanish climber Iñaki Ochoa de Olza and his Romanian climbing partner Horia Colibàšanu had gotten stuck at 7400 meters. Iñaki was apparently suffering altitude illness and unable to move.

Simon and I started out that night in an attempt to rescue the two climbers, who were about 3200 meters above us.

Two days later Simon, who had climbed to Camp 3 with me, took the altitude-sick Romanian under his wing and descended with him. I rushed up to Camp 4, where I found Iñaki in his tent. He was in extremely bad condition. Even though I spent the night injecting drugs, feeding him, and giving him water, his condition worsened by the minute. In the early morning he stopped breathing. I was able to resuscitate him once, but then it was over. There was nothing I could do for Iñaki but be by his side.

After I struggled down in heavy snowfall and zero visibility, Simon and I returned home as quickly as possible. Continuing our expedition was completely out of the question after what we had just experienced. At least Horia was alive, but Iñaki's death and how he had died really got me thinking. I started to question a few things. For the time being, I was fed up with the South Face of Annapurna.

Even though I managed to not think about Annapurna, I was still fascinated by the idea of soloing big walls at a good speed. I started a phase during which I concentrated on perfecting technical skills needed for solo and speed climbs while making the most of my physical fitness. My speed records on the north faces of the Eiger, Grandes Jorasses, Matterhorn, and Les Droites were a consequence of this training. The next step was transferring these skills to the big walls in the Himalaya, where I had to adjust my speed to the different conditions, such as the thinner air and maximum exposure. Ascending quickly and spending as little time in the death zone as possible was a safety factor.

My goal was to climb 8000-meter peaks as efficiently as possible, and to achieve this I needed more practice at extreme altitudes. In 2009 I got my first experience above 8000 meters on Gasherbrum II and Makalu. In 2011 I soloed a combination of three existing routes on the South Face of Shishapangma and scaled Cho Oyu, and I reached the top of Everest via the normal route the following year.

Slowly but surely, I felt ready to give the South Face of Annapurna another go. The temptation was still there, and in 2013 the time had come to take on this challenge for the third time.

▲ ▲ ▲

Given the height of the South Face of Annapurna, I concentrated on endurance training. After my return from Everest I spent the first two months doing a lot of trail running. As I had done many times before, I ran up the Niesen, a mountain in my home region near Lake Thun. During these sessions I would run up to the top three times, 1700 meters of elevation gain per rotation. This was physically and mentally very challenging. When I started the first rotation, I knew that I had three grueling rounds ahead of me. The only thing to do was blank out that thought and just run as relaxed as possible. Once I reached the top I took the funicular back down. The second time I would run faster, even though my legs were burning. The first part of the run was the most difficult, as the path from the station started off quite steeply. Later I'd try to speed up, which took some effort because my legs were tired. I would try hard to keep my upper body upright and let my legs do their thing. Suddenly I'd find my rhythm again, and my legs felt as if they were running on their own. The ride back down to the valley on the funicular always interrupted my concentration, and I'd start to wonder: "How is it going to be this time around?" Once down I would immediately start running again. The third rotation was always the easiest, as I knew it would be the last. After I'd run the three rotations, 5100 meters of elevation gain, the shower at the top station always felt like heaven.

Training like this also made me mentally stronger. It put the big Himalayan walls into perspective: at 2500 meters the

South Face of Annapurna was suddenly reduced to being only half as tall as three times the Niesen. The same applied to the North Face of the Eiger. With its mere 1700 meters one could almost be tempted to climb it thrice in a day. For me, training was never a burden. I loved it, and rarely did I not feel like training and have to push myself to go out. After a hard session I felt much more content than after a gentle mountain climb. In the evenings I loved feeling my heavy legs and arms that were threatening to burst.

On July 20, 2013, I took part in the Eiger Ultra Trail race. The weather could not have been more perfect, and I utterly enjoyed the run, which covered 51 kilometers and 3100 meters of elevation gain. From Grindelwald the route went up to the Grosse Scheidegg, where the first food station was located. It continued via the First to the Schynige Platte before it descended to Burglauenen. It was technically challenging. The descent was steep, the path was narrow, and the terrain was rough and rocky. For me, this was the perfect running ground, and I could accelerate to my heart's content. I was particularly happy to make such good progress from Grindelwald to Burglauenen. Even though my legs were getting heavy, they were still moving smoothly, which is something I often struggle with on the flat. I hardly ever train on flat terrain, and when I get tired then I seem to come to a complete halt and not make any progress at all. But this was the perfect run. I was able to reach my physical limits but still have a smile on my face when I reached the finish line after a little more than six hours. I felt inspired and energized by the presence of all the other runners.

I love the atmosphere all the events. With so many people around me, it is the opposite of what I usually look for in the mountains. Everyone is prepared to give their personal best. Even though your legs are burning, you keep on running because if the person in front of you can do it, you can too. You understand each other without exchanging a word. Everyone is working hard, and, despite all the pain, everyone is enthusiastic. The people cheering you on and all the helpers providing you with food and drink are also a huge part of the special atmosphere. I feel good in these surroundings. These are the positive moments that make me happy. And if I have to struggle through them, they will stay with me even longer.

At one point, though, I was fed up with running, and to keep up my motivation I looked for an alpine goal that would give me pleasure and put my training to the test. I had been thinking about soloing and traversing the Grandes Jorasses in the Mont Blanc region for quite some time, and now the time had come. I was planning to start from Chamonix, climb nonstop, and descend to Courmayeur. I got very excited about the idea.

Unfortunately Nicole could not share my enthusiasm about my latest plan. While we sipped red wine at our dining table, the conversation went around in circles. I tried to make her understand that the technical difficulties of traversing the Grandes Jorasses were not a problem for me at all. I said I would not climb for speed and would put in protection in case the conditions got difficult. My arguments did not convince her. Of course, I could understand Nicole's worries since climbing solo always bears a certain risk. If something happened, I would be alone, with nobody there to help me. My abilities and concentration comprised the only safety net I would have.

I had actually promised Nicole that I would stop doing solo climbs, but this did not change the fact that days I spend in the mountains on my own are the most beautiful and most impressive days for me. There is nothing else, just the mountain and me, and that's what I love. There is nobody to whom I have to justify anything. I can make my own decisions and do what I want. These are my most precious times. I feel at my best when I can just walk, climb, or run. I get into a beautiful rhythm, and nothing can interrupt it.

Nicole knows me well, and she knows my abilities. When I provide her with more details about my plans, she can better understand them. For me, Grade VI climbs are nothing much. The chances of me falling are pretty slim, but of course they are never zero. One can slip and fall on easy ground as Nicole did a couple of years ago—she was very lucky to have survived. Mountaineers have to accept a risk. No matter how well prepared, when you climb a mountain you always run the risk of something unexpected happening. Maybe this is exactly what makes mountaineering so fascinating. The Swiss avalanche expert Werner Munter once said that taking risks is a basic human right: everyone has the right to take risks, but to what extent is up to each individual. Before I decide whether I have enough experience and training to realize a plan without taking an unacceptable risk, I try to evaluate it realistically and judge my abilities critically.

In the end Nicole came up with a convincing argument against the Grandes Jorasses project. The approach march was long, and a large part of it went across a glacier. Crossing a glacier alone and without a rope is dangerous, especially in the summer without skis. Crevasses are unpredictable, and you can easily fall in when the snow collapses. Nicole and I once experienced this together when we traversed from the Schreckhorn to the Lauteraarhorn in the Bernese Oberland. At 4:00 a.m., when it was still pitch black, we roped up to cross the glacier. I was leading the way, following an existing track, with Nicole coming up behind me on the rope. Suddenly I came across a huge crevasse. I had to make a big step to get to the other side, where the tracks from the previous day were visible. I put my right foot exactly into the existing footprint, but when I put my weight on it I plunged into the crevasse. Even though it was still cold in the early morning hours, the snow bridge had collapsed. On this occasion it was not a problem. Nicole was able to hold me on the rope, and I could easily climb out of the crevasse. But without a rope I would have probably disappeared forever.

Compared to glacier crossings, climbing is less risky, as it is more calculable and controllable. For this reason, Nicole and I agreed that it would be better for me to find a project that did not involve a glacier crossing. The result of this discussion was the idea of traversing the entire Peuterey ridge on the south side of Mont Blanc. Starting in the Italian valley of Val Veny, the ridge leads via the Aiguille Noire and the Aiguille Blanche de Peuterey all the way to the summit of Mont Blanc. The Peuterey Intégral is considered the longest ridge in the Alps, and if you add the descent down to Chamonix, it is probably on par with the Grandes Jorasses. I was happy that Nicole and I had found a compromise we both could live with. These discussions would probably always come up in my relationship with Nicole, and I knew that I had to avoid being too selfish or too insistent on doing my own thing. On the other hand, it wouldn't be good for either of us if I only went along and felt that I was no longer living my own life. In the long run this wouldn't make either of us happy.

The south ridge to the Aiguille Noire de Peuterey, which is a pleasant fifty-pitch granite climb (up to Grade V+) leading via numerous rocky towers to 3772 meters, marks the beginning of the Peuterey Intégral. It is followed by a long rappel of 450 meters that gets you down to the Dames Anglaises, from which you traverse across to the Aiguille Blanche de Peuterey. Once you have reached its 4112-meter summit you continue to the Col de Peuterey before you gain the classic Peuterey ridge and climb all the way to the top of Mont Blanc. Getting to the highest point at 4810 meters involves ascending another 1500 vertical meters, with climbing sections in the lower Grade IV. This is a proper alpine undertaking, which has its grand finale on a 50-degree ice and snow slope. As I wanted to start straight from the valley floor without spending a night at the Borelli refuge, I added an extra elevation gain of 1000 meters. In plain numbers this meant ascending 1000 meters on the approach, climbing another 4500 meters on the ridge, and descending 3800 meters.

Karl Brendel and Hermann Schaller made the first ascent of the south ridge of the Aiguille Noire in 1930. It took them two days to complete this feat. Traversing the whole ridge all the way to the summit of Mont Blanc like I was planning to do had first been done by Germans Richard Hechtel and Günther Kittelmann in July 1953. It took them three full days. Nowadays, two days to climb the whole ridge should be sufficient depending on the speed and abilities of the climbers, but most rope parties need two bivouacs. The small Craveri Bivouac is at the Brèches des Dames Anglaises, near the dramatic northern notch. It is really tiny and only allows you to sit or lie down, but it is well protected from adverse weather. There were also faster rope parties, such as the two Italians Matteo Pellin and Arnaud Clavel. It only took them twenty-eight hours from Val Veny to the summit and back to the Gonella refuge and Courmayeur. And Slovenian climber Luka Lindič had reached the top of Mont Blanc from the Borelli refuge in fifteen hours just a few weeks before I started my Peuterey Intégral project.

I felt extremely motivated, but it was a serious undertaking, and I had to study it. I had never been to the south side of Mont Blanc before. With Caroline George, a Swiss mountain guide who lives near Chamonix, I went on a fact-finding mission. Caroline and I had known each other for years but had not climbed together for a long time. She is always up for a good climb, and the Peuterey Intégral was a good excuse to do something together again.

Unfortunately we could not find the route we wanted to do, but after my reconnaissance with Caroline I was convinced that it would be possible for me to solo the ridge. The only thing I needed now was good weather, and I needed it quickly since Nicole and I were due to go to Canada five days later, on August 17. Fortunately the weather gods were on my side, and the weather window was forecast to stay open for a while.

On August 12 I returned to Chamonix and set up my base camp at the Les Bossons campsite. I chose to stay in a tent rather than at a friend's house since I wanted to be on my own. In the afternoon I traveled to Courmayeur and continued to Val Veny to find out how to best proceed logistically. Matteo Pellin, one of the two Courmayeur mountain guides who had climbed the ridge, managed the campsite in Peuterey. He invited me to stay with him, and since this was the perfect starting point for me, I gladly accepted. I drove back through the Mont Blanc tunnel to Les Bossons and returned to my tent. The following day I took the bus to the south side of the mountain, where one of Matteo's friends picked me up in Courmayeur. The campsite Monte Bianco la Sorgente in Val Veny turned out to be a paradise. There were grassy spots for tents, and visitors could also stay in old stone houses that had clearly been renovated with a lot of love and passion.

In the afternoon I jogged up the 1000 meters to the start of the south ridge. It was good to blow away the cobwebs and get to know the way since I would start in the dark the following morning. I deposited my backpack at the bottom of the ridge, which would save me having to carry anything in the morning. I had only taken the bare minimum. A

60-meter Dynema rope with a diameter of 6 millimeters, my harness for rappelling, a few carabiners and slings, a helmet, climbing boots, crampons, and ice axes were the basics. I also had gloves, a hat, sunglasses, a thin down jacket, and hard-shell trousers and jacket to protect myself in case the weather should turn, which can always happen in the high Alps. Water would probably be sufficiently available on the way, and I thought that five energy gels and four bars would be sufficient food.

Before I set out, Matteo and his friends spoiled me with a delicious dinner. I gobbled down the pasta as if there were no tomorrow. I certainly needed the carbohydrates for the following day. I was relaxed, enjoyed the Italian hospitality, and was excited about starting my new project. Before dessert was served one of Matteo's friends suddenly came up with the idea to film the climb. He said that Matteo, being a helicopter rescuer, would probably have good connections to allow him to go up in a helicopter and film. He was so excited that I could not get a word in edgewise. But Matteo got in a word, and it was simply "no." This suited me just fine. I wanted to go climbing, and I wanted to do it for myself, not for anyone else. A helicopter buzzing above me all the time would have ruined my experience. I was relieved that Matteo thought along the same lines. There was no further discussion, and I did not have to justify my wishes. I might not make it to the summit anyway. One never knows.

At the crack of dawn on August 14, Matteo, who had insisted on getting up at 4:00 a.m. with me, said goodbye after having made me delicious coffee. The biscotti that came with the coffee wouldn't provide much energy, but I felt well fed, and it was too early in the morning to eat much more anyway. I headed out, and at ten minutes past five I reached my backpack at the bottom of the ridge. I had already done the first 1000 meters of elevation, and faster than I had anticipated. The world around me was still pitch black, but I started to climb anyway. This was exactly the same spot Caroline and I had set out from a week earlier. We had also climbed in the dark, so I was convinced that I would find the way again this time.

Slowly day began breaking, and climbing became increasingly fun with the light. It was reassuring to see the cracks, gullies, and spikes I was holding on to. I felt comfortable on this terrain. After I reached the tower of the Pointe Welzenbach, I took a short break to change from mountaineering boots into rock-climbing shoes before I rappelled 25 meters. The route was technically not that difficult, and I could have easily continued in my big mountain boots, but I moved more efficiently and safely in rock-climbing shoes, an important consideration given that I was climbing without a rope.

After having rappelled into the notch, I was faced with the first serious section on a slab with very few handholds. I had to completely rely on the friction and grip of my rubber soles. Once I had negotiated that section, the route continued vertically toward a dihedral. I had warmed up now, and I moved without stopping. It felt free and easy. From the Pointe Brendel I descended east toward another notch, where I veered to the left to gain a chimney, which was still in the shade. The Pointe Ottoz towered menacingly above me. I remembered that I had to step out of the chimney to the left and gain the wall via a short steep section. The face was precipitous and exposed. Given the 400 meters opening up below me, I was very grateful for the solid handholds and footholds. I climbed the west side of the ridge until I reached an overhang. From there I traversed right toward the east, which brought me back to the sunny side of the ridge. The tower started to lean back somewhat, which made climbing all the way to the Pointe Ottoz relatively easy.

From this tower the top of the Aiguille Noire did not seem very far, but my progress still dragged on for a while. Right under the sixth tower, the Pointe Bich, I came across another difficult section that required climbing a crack. Three powerful moves got me over the edge to the tower, from which I continued without great difficulties to the top of the Aiguille Noire, which I reached at 8:30 a.m.

Even though the sun was not yet very high, I could feel its wonderful warmth. I was very excited to have most of the day ahead of me. For *znüni*—a second breakfast, which the Swiss usually have when they are at work—I treated myself to an energy bar. I remained on the summit for a while to soak up the beauty, sitting next to a metal Madonna statue that must get struck by lightning frequently, given the number of holes in it. *It must be really harsh up here during a thunderstorm*, I thought. I was lucky and let the sun shine on my face and enjoyed the peace and quiet. I did not feel under pressure. At this rate I would easily reach the summit of Mont Blanc in good time. I always feel relaxed when I am moving on my own: easy, uncomplicated, and efficient.

When I left the summit there was a bit of lightning in the south, but the sky above me was completely clear. Humidity was low, but I was expecting the Bise, which is a cold dry wind from the northeast, to bring some cumulus clouds later in the day. Having absorbed the beauty of the surroundings, I began the long rappel to the rocky towers of the Dames Anglaises. Down there I was back in the shade, which immediately felt chilly. Bit by bit, I rappelled all sixteen pitches. I had to improvise occasionally, as the pitches were 50 meters long. With a single 60-meter rope, I could only rappel 30 meters at a time. I set up my own belays, which were not always foolproof. I had adjusted my entire rappelling system to the 6-millimeter cord I used to save weight. Using such a thin rope requires a special rappelling device with sufficient braking resistance, otherwise you gather too much speed or get hot fingers. I was using an old Petzl Reversino. This small and light rappelling device was no longer available on the market but still worked perfectly well. It is not really suitable for normal ropes, but it was ideal for my purpose. I had also adjusted my safety system using a Prusik loop, which had a diameter of only 4 millimeters and was also attached to the cord. My rappelling system looked more like a children's toy than a safety device, but it worked fine and weighed next to nothing.

A broken gully led me to a traverse marking the start of the descent to the Schneider Couloir, which I followed to climb back up to the Craveri Bivouac. The rock was pretty brittle here, and I felt much more comfortable climbing such classic alpine terrain on my own. A roped party would not have been able to secure this route sufficiently, and with more people on the route the danger of falling rocks is a lot higher. I did not have to take care of anyone and could climb at my own speed and my own rhythm. This day it was just me and the mountain, nothing else. It couldn't have been more perfect.

Just below the Pointe Gugliermina, I heard voices. A roped party was climbing above me. When I overtook them, the second roped party of the day, I stayed well clear of the two climbers so I would not endanger them if I kicked off any rocks. They were going at their own speed, the right speed for them.

I stopped to fill my water bottles. The sun was shining, and the ice and snow were melting, which provided me with enough water. I could drink to my heart's content and not run the risk of dehydrating on this long route. I continued up through a wide gully. As anticipated, a few clouds had formed by now. It got colder, but I was still well away from the cloud cover.

On the southeast summit of the Aiguille Blanche, I put on my mountaineering boots and crampons. I was now moving on snow. The sharp ridge led to the Pointe Central, where I had to rappel again. After three rappels and one climbing section, I reached the Col de Peuterey. Thick clouds had now formed around me, and visibility was probably less than two meters. This made finding the traverse to the Grand Pilier d'Angle more difficult. I traversed back and forth three times to find a possible way to continue. It took me about thirty minutes before I decided to just give it a go. I did not have a choice, and I was feeling a bit tense. I only had a few pieces of hardware, and if I got lost I would end up in a dead-end situation pretty quickly. But I was lucky and reached the Grand Pilier d'Angle without any problems. At 4243 meters I was once again above the clouds, and the summit of Mont Blanc did not seem far away. Up here I found a few old tracks. They would have been very useful down at the Col de Peuterey!

I started to feel tired, which was not surprising since I had been on the move for quite some time. My gloves had been wet, and now at an elevation of more than 4000 meters they were frozen. I decided not to change into my spare gloves, though. I would put them on when I reached the summit in order to have dry gloves for the descent. Every once in a while I had to stop to warm my hands. As soon as blood flowed back into my fingers, I continued. Now I really appreciated the warmth of my mountaineering boots. In the run-up to this climb, I had contemplated doing the whole route in my running shoes, as this would have saved me a lot of weight. On the lower section on the Aiguille Noire, where I was wearing my climbing shoes, it would have been easier to have light running shoes instead of the heavy mountain boots in my backpack. But as expected, there was more ice than snow up here, and I would have had difficulties finding a good grip with the light crampons I have for my running shoes. And my mountaineering boots did not really weigh that much. They had been made to my specifications and were about 100 grams (3.5 ounces) lighter than the super-lightweight boots one can buy on the market. But no matter how good they were, they could not prevent my calves from burning when I put all my weight on my front points. I felt relieved when I reached the summit of Mont Blanc de Courmayeur at three in the afternoon. I was all by myself, there was not a breath of wind in the air, and I was above the clouds. It was sensational. I utterly enjoyed this moment, which was entirely mine. Having ascended so quickly, I was convinced that I would be able to get down to the valley the same day. Even though fatigue was slowly creeping in, I was still feeling strong. It was reassuring to know that I was fast. I did not have to rush and did not feel under pressure. It was already past 3:30 p.m. when I traversed across to Mont Blanc's main summit and started my descent toward the Dôme du Goûter. The track along the normal route was well trodden, which allowed me to break into a jog on the downhill. Far below me I could see Chamonix. It was still very far. Around 3800 meters of elevation plus quite a distance on the route along the Dôme du Goûter separated me from my destination. I was not worried about it, but slowly I started to feel my thigh muscles as I jogged. On this terrain my running shoes with light crampons would have been much better—I would have been able to roll off my front foot more easily and use less energy—but one has to make compromises.

From the Vallot Hut the route flattened out, with only a small climb at the end leading toward the Dôme du Goûter. I passed another roped party. Both climbers seemed absolutely exhausted, and I asked them whether I could be of any help. They declined and said that they were simply tired. *They'll be fine*, I thought, convinced that they would later be proud of their accomplishment. Beyond the Goûter Hut I was not sure where to continue, but it did not take too long to find the turnoff. The path led past the old hut. I was now below the snowline on a route fixed with chains and other safety equipment. It was fun running downhill even though my legs were getting increasingly tired. The valley floor came closer at a very slow rate. Below the Tête Rousse Hut, I came across a signpost. I was happy to see that the sign did not indicate the walking time, as I didn't really want to know how far I still had to go. At Bellevue, another sign told me that it was still two hours and twenty minutes to get to Les Houches. It would have been perfect running ground, but it was almost impossible in my mountaineering boots.

I reached the church in Les Houches just after 8:00 p.m, a little over sixteen hours after I had bid goodbye to Matteo at the campsite in Val Veny. I contemplated having something to eat here, but even though I was ravenously hungry I decided to carry on. I wanted to get to my tent and my car in Les Bossons. I toyed with the idea of calling someone to come and pick me up, but as it was such a lovely evening I decided to walk back to Les Bossons.

About an hour later I sat next to my tent. Then I indulged in a hot shower and a carbohydrate drink before I finally lay down. My hunger had disappeared, and all I wanted to do was curl up in my sleeping bag. I sent Matteo a text message to let him know that I was all right and that I had arrived safe and sound in the other valley. I had had an amazing day. I finally fell asleep with a big smile on my face.

▲ ▲ ▲

After this dress rehearsal for Annapurna, I felt well prepared for the autumn season. The Canadian climber Don Bowie would be my partner on this climb. Weather and conditions permitting, we wanted to scale the South Face, otherwise we would defer to the east ridge.

I had met Don five years previously, in 2008, when I was climbing Annapurna with Simon Anthamatten. Don had been part of Iñaki Ochoa de Olza's expedition but had left before the ill-fated summit attempt due to disagreements within the team. He had gone back to Kathmandu, but when he heard about Iñaki's distress, he had immediately returned to base camp by helicopter. Together with Denis Urubko he climbed up carrying a few bottles of oxygen while I was fighting for Iñaki's life at 7400 meters. Unfortunately their ascent was hampered by deep snow, and they did not make it in time. Iñaki died before the oxygen could reach him.

A year later Don's path and mine crossed again in Pakistan, where we were at the same base camp. Don was attempting Gasherbrum III, while Nicole and I were climbing Gasherbrum II. During long periods of bad weather we discovered that we shared a profound love of coffee.

In 2011 we climbed together for the first time. We started off on Shishapangma and then climbed Cho Oyu and Everest. My summit day on Cho Oyu was pretty bad, as I was suffering from diarrhea and had zero energy. At about 8000 meters I had more or less decided to turn back and give it another go the following day. At exactly that moment Don caught up with me and encouraged me to carry on to the summit. He just wouldn't let me turn back. Even though he comes across a bit cool at times, he is a very sensitive guy who would do anything for a friend. He is pretty quiet, and I don't know many people like him. We found that we had a mutual understanding that did not require any words. This is pretty crucial when on a big expedition where you spend months in cramped conditions and it is almost impossible to keep out of each other's way. In addition, his training is very similar to mine. He very deliberately prepares himself for an expedition. He is big and strong, and at first glance he looks more like an athlete than a mountaineer. He had scaled K2, Gasherbrum I, and Cho Oyu, and he was familiar with high altitude and knew how his body reacted to it. I was convinced that if Don told me that he wanted to join my expedition to the South Face of Annapurna, then he was confident that he could do it.

In mid-September 2013 I traveled with photographer Dan Patitucci and his wife, Janine, via Doha to Kathmandu. We stayed at the small, no-frills Hotel Manaslu, which has inefficient service but a good price. It also has a pretty garden that is tended daily. At this time of year its flowers were a colorful explosion. Pierre Béghin and Jean-Christophe Lafaille had used the same hotel in 1992. In 2013 we stayed in Kathmandu only long enough to run all the necessary errands. I could not wait to get to the mountain. Finally Annapurna had become real again!

Kathmandu was quite familiar to me. I had been there so many times that it had almost lost the exotic character it had for me during my first visit. I always enjoyed going back there, and I liked that I now knew my way around the city. First and foremost, however, I had to deal with all the bureaucracy that comes with such an expedition. The meeting at the Ministry of Tourism was always a mere formality. For the officials involved it was mainly a money-making exercise. They always came up with new regulations and absurd permits requiring mountaineers to dig deeper into their pockets. I played along, paid my dues, and simply went climbing.

Don wanted to produce a documentary about Annapurna, and Jonah Mathewson was supposed to film it. Don, Jonah, and I, together with Dan and Janine, took a small plane to

Pokhara, Nepal's second-biggest city. Our cook, Kaji, had already taken most of our gear to base camp a week earlier and had pitched the tents and set up the kitchen. After one night in Pokhara, we took a minibus to Nayapul, where we transferred to a jeep taking us along the Modi Kola River to Kimche. With their newly constructed roads, the Nepali authorities had saved us a whole trekking day. One could argue about whether the road construction is a blessing or a curse. Of course, trekkers on the Annapurna Circuit would rather hike through untouched nature. On the other hand, you can't blame the Nepalese for wanting to expand their road network. Just like us Westerners, they want to be more mobile. I did not object to having one less trekking day. I wanted to get to the mountain as quickly as possible. One less day of trekking meant one more day of climbing.

In oppressive heat we hiked to Ginu. We were going to stay the night there and visit the beautiful hot springs nearby. The forest was dense, and there was no sign of big mountains. The heat was almost unbearable, but despite the humidity, we still walked to the hot springs. Once we had immersed our bodies in the hot water, a thunderstorm arrived, the skies opened, and it poured down rain relentlessly. We had no intention of getting out of the water and walking back to the lodge in the downpour. The atmosphere was threatening, and it almost seemed we had reached the end of the world. It was dark, with a pitch-black sky, and the roaring Modi Kola thundered next to us. In the end we did not manage to sit out the rain; our empty stomachs drove us back to the lodge. When we got there we were absolutely soaked and had to change into dry clothes before sitting down for dinner.

The following morning I decided to go all the way to base camp. I could no longer wait to see the South Face, and it would also be good training to run a longish distance just before the expedition. The rest of the group would walk and get there a day later. I headed out with the team on September 21 but said farewell in Chomrong and started to run. It felt good. I ran up the valley through the forest without any difficulty, gaining 2900 meters of elevation and covering 21 kilometers to get to base camp. At midday I reached base camp after about six hours of running. The mountains were engulfed in thick clouds. Annapurna was hiding, but it was still good to have arrived.

I was excited to see Kaji again. We had not met for more than a year, and I was looking forward to having a cup of sweet, milky Nepali tea with him. We had been through a lot together. He had been part of my very first expedition in 2005, when I was doing the so-called Khumbu Express. I will never forget when he came up to meet me on top of the Cho La Pass. I had soloed the North Face of Cholatse and descended into another valley, which meant that I needed to climb up the 5400-meter Cho La to get back. It was the third day of my expedition, I had long ago run out of provisions, and I was starving and absolutely exhausted. At the foot of the pass, I asked a trekker if he could give me something to eat, and he told me he did not have anything to spare. Maybe he would have softened had I told him where I was coming from and how long I had been on the go, but I let it be. Another trekker was kind enough to give me a chocolate bar, which I devoured just before I started the ascent. Had I only known that there was a lodge an hour's walk in the other direction, I would have gone there. But then I would have missed that unforgettable moment on the pass, when Kaji suddenly appeared, handing me cookies and a big thermos of tea. These were the most delicious cookies and the best tea in my life! This had been eight years ago, and since that time Kaji had brought me tea and cookies on many occasions. He had always looked out for me and seemed to know exactly when I was coming back.

He always made sure to be there and to give me tea and cookies. Kaji had become a sort of symbol for me: whenever I spotted him, I was on the summit. I had reached my goal.

Annapurna base camp was on grassy ground. That fall of 2013, Kaji had set it up right behind the lodges and not on the other side of the moraine as in previous years. Logistically this was easier and, as it turned out, was closer to the start of the climb. At base camp we were using new tents that were big enough to stand up in. I'd had them made in Nepal the previous year. They were yellow, and our camp looked like an Asterix and Obelix comic with the mess tent, the kitchen tent, and the three sleeping tents all lined up. We even had the luxury of having camping beds rather than sleeping mats on the ground. Dendi, the owner of the trekking agency, had come up with this. I had no clue where he had found the beds, but I did not complain. The mess tent was equipped with a heater, but it was too warm to use it. As the days were getting increasingly colder, though, it would be useful before long. The days were short in the fall, and it got dark pretty early. With no electric lights or heater, the nights become unbearably long since everyone crawls into their sleeping bags as soon as the sun goes down. Over the years I have learned that climbers should be allowed some luxury. It is certainly good for our motivation.

At the crack of dawn the following day, I left base camp for advanced base camp. We had planned to set it up at the foot of the South Face at about 5000 meters, which was about an hour and a half below the start of the climb. I took a few bamboo rods to mark the route and followed the same way I had taken in previous years. I crossed the glacier and stepped onto the moraine and the grassy slopes on the other side. Then I walked past the old base camp and descended back onto the glacier. With rope and the few ice screws I had taken, I wanted to fix the icefall for everyone to go up and down independently, without having to rely on another person.

The icefall was in pretty dire condition that year. I spent a lot of time finding a good route, which was important since we would use it many times on this expedition. It was definitely worth investing time and effort to fix a good route. When it had gotten quite late, I stopped halfway through the icefall to return to base camp. The first day had been very productive. I felt a lot calmer, and the South Face looked magnificent. Back at camp Kaji informed me that the glacier had changed so much that it was no longer necessary to make the detour on the right side of the moraine: it was now possible to go through the center. He could have told me in the morning! I had spent all day wondering why there were markings in the middle of the glacier.

In the meantime the others had arrived. Don, Jonah, Dan, and Janine were busy settling into their tents while I was already on the mountain in my thoughts. I wanted to set up advanced base camp as quickly as possible in order to be ready for the climb. It was important for Don and me to make use of any stretch of good weather and get onto the face as soon as possible. The following day I rested and sorted our gear. I was trying to establish what should go up immediately and what could remain below. The next day I climbed up again, this time taking the route through the center moraine, just as Kaji had told me. It was certainly a lot better. In the upper section of the icefall, I took quite some time to fix the rope on the steep sections. I was able to find a pretty good and safe way through the crevasses. Out of curiosity I continued to advanced base camp to find out how much snow there was. I was pleasantly surprised that there was none at all. Fantastic! It would be a comfortable camp, and I had already done the first section of the climb.

The following day we prepared everything: rope, equipment, food. It was crucial to have enough provisions at advanced base camp to allow us to stay there for a while. This was a tactical decision. After having been on so many expeditions, I had gotten to know myself pretty well, and I knew that if I didn't have enough provisions, at advanced base camp, I would rather go down to base camp and spend less time acclimatizing at 5000 meters. At 4200 meters our base camp was relatively low, which was good for recovery but not high enough for acclimatizing properly so I really wanted to spend a few nights at our advanced base camp. It was in a beautiful spot, right below the glacier. The view was even more stunning than from base camp. Here we were surrounded by steep, imposing faces. At the moment, though, all the gear still had to be carried up from base camp. We had just started, but my thoughts were already a step ahead, as was often the case. I felt very optimistic. I was focused and busy, and my gut feeling was that it would work out this time around.

Don needed some more time for acclimatization. I stayed at base camp for a few nights and used the days to carry our gear up to advanced base camp. The team spirit was great, and everyone lent a hand. Our Sherpas Nima and Tenji helped us set up advanced base camp and carry loads. Dan, the photographer, offered to carry up another load with me. It turned out to be a long and exhausting day for him. He was not properly acclimatized, and we took a long time for the descent. It was getting dark when we approached base camp, and the last section was a small climb back up the moraine. Even though it was only 100 meters, this felt endless after such a hard day. Kaji's dinner, which alternated between pasta and French fries with vegetables, tasted even more delicious after such a day.

The following day I returned to advanced base camp and stayed a night. Spending this first night at 5000 meters got me even more excited. I had only been here for five days and was already a step closer to my goal. Don was planning to come up the next day. For dinner I prepared my new favorite mountain meal, the traditional Swiss rösti. Together with some onion and Parmesan cheese, the ready-made potatoes turned out to be a true gourmet dinner. Not particularly light to carry but absolutely worth the effort! At this altitude, I could afford to carry a bit more weight, and good food was essential. I had also brought a comfortable double-walled tent. It got dark pretty early, and before long I crawled into my sleeping bag. I tried to read a few pages, but concentrating was difficult, and I soon fell asleep. On expeditions I have a lot of time to sleep, which I absolutely love. I adapt to nature, which means that once it gets light I get up, and when it gets dark I withdraw into my tent. It's as simple as that.

The next day was beautiful, with the sun already warming me in the early morning hours. After coffee and a bite to eat, I headed out toward the start of the climb carrying a few bamboo sticks. I pretty much knew the way but had no idea how much the glacier had changed. I started out following my route of 2007 and 2008, which headed straight out of the camp and then veered left over some scree. I came across a few old way markers and cairns pointing to the glacier. I walked slowly, step by step: there was no pressure. Today was just about finding a good route and putting in markers. Once on the glacier I tried to spot the most direct path through the crevasses. I marked the dangers with two bamboo sticks each, one on each side of the crevasse. Two sticks relatively close together indicated danger. Without gaining much height I traversed to the right until I reached the center of the glacier. From there I thought it would be possible to climb up to the bergschrund. Here the glacier was not as rugged and had fewer crevasses, but higher up I spotted a huge crevasse. It had been there in 2008, and I remembered going around it to the right. I turned right and found that the rest of the way to the bergschrund was free of crevasses. Suddenly I found myself standing below the start of the climb. A steep snowy flank reached all the way up to a small rock barrier, and I looked for a good place to climb it. Five years earlier the glacier had reached all the way to the face, but now a 20-meter band of rock was exposed that we would need to negotiate. Fortunately I had brought a 5-millimeter cord to fix this steep section, which would later allow us to easily climb it fairly quickly. The hot sun was beating down, and water was running down the rock. I found it hard to motivate myself to tackle this section. The rock looked steep and wet, and the idea of taking a shower up here at 5650 meters was not appealing, but I set out regardless. The rock was almost vertical, but there were good holds for hands and feet. Despite the shower, it was actually fun to do some rock climbing again. I first climbed over a small pillar that ended in a dihedral, where the rock leaned back and flattened out somewhat. Now the climbing felt less exhausting. The last 2 meters were almost vertical before I traversed to the left.

I reached the upper edge of the rocky step, where it was a lot flatter. I actually managed to walk upright. After a while I found a solid rock, which I used as an anchor. I put a sling around it, fed the rope through, looked around for a while, and then started to rappel. I felt happy and content. I'd had a good day: I had reached a new high point, and at 5650 meters I was feeling great and did not have the slightest sign of a headache. The way to the wall had been opened. Lower down I set up another fixed point. I jammed a bolt into a crack just above the small pillar, attached a carabiner, and clipped the rope through. From there I rappelled straight down to the snowfield. Then I retraced my steps across the glacier and was back at advanced base camp before I knew it.

Step by step, I was getting closer to Annapurna. The time I spent on the mountain gave me the opportunity to familiarize myself with it. Slowly but surely, we established a sort of friendship. The face became more structured, and I could see what to expect. Everything became more tangible: the rock, the snow, and the distances. Everything about the South Face of Annapurna used to be based on assumptions, but now it had become real.

The following day was a rest day. Don had arrived the previous evening. The weather was still brilliant, and I found it hard to sit still. I was full of energy, but we were forced to remain at advanced base camp for a couple of days to get our bodies acclimatized. We enjoyed hanging out at the base of the South Face of Annapurna, just the two of us. It was sensational: The weather was holding, and the temperatures were incredibly warm. I was already convinced that climbing in the Himalaya in the fall was, overall, better than in the spring.

After my fourth night at 5000 meters, we decided to climb higher. Don and I set out leisurely in the morning. We did not have too many plans for the day but intended to set up a camp at around 6000 meters that would serve as a good point from which to advance farther on the face. Béghin and Lafaille had put their first camp somewhere up there, and it seemed that there was a protected spot on a rocky ledge. We followed the marked way to the start of the climb, and despite our heavy backpacks we were able to negotiate the ledge relatively easily and continue to climb without a rope. I was in front, and Don was a short distance behind me. Every once in a while I waited for him, and then we took a few pictures and continued up on firm snow.

At about 6100 meters at the left on top of the rocks, we found an ideal spot for a camp. It was a real eagle's nest and required some work. Digging out a platform and flattening the ground with rocks and snow, we both felt quite cheerful and relaxed. In addition to a lightweight tent, I had brought its vestibule, which added another 400 grams (14 ounces) to my load but would afford a lot more space. It was better to cook in the vestibule rather than inside the tent, where condensation is always a problem. As the temperature difference between outside and inside is much greater with a single-walled tent, condensation forms, making the tent and everything inside it damp. During the night, the condensation freezes, and if you are not careful when you stretch in the morning, it covers you in small snow crystals.

We used the rest of the fixed rope, which we had found at our campsite, to anchor the tent and make it stormproof. I was surprised to find relatively new and good ropes up here, and Don mentioned a Japanese expedition that had been here recently. I had not heard anything about it. In the late afternoon, when the sun had gone down and cool air had moved in, we were already tucked up in our sleeping bags. Such moments in the mountains are special. We were at 6100 meters on the South Face of Annapurna, and night was falling. The stars were shining brightly, far more brightly than back home. I felt much closer to the sky, and the stars seemed more tangible than in the Alps. We fell asleep early. The night was long, but I slept soundly.

In the dim light of dawn, I carefully stuck my nose out of my sleeping bag. It was cold and damp, and I could hardly bring myself to get up. I was dying for coffee, however, and I finally started melting some snow. Don had brought packets of Starbucks instant coffee from the States. This tastes like the real deal and is a treat for your taste buds at high camp. Don and I were in agreement: There is nothing better than a cup of coffee in the morning.

After breakfast I got restless and needed to move. I wanted to climb a little bit higher to have a look at the conditions on the face, while Don would stay at camp. He had not slept well and was complaining about a headache. It was warm as I climbed the rocky ledge right behind our tent. I knew from Lafaille's book that he and Béghin had fixed some rope here in 1992. The climb was steep, but it was going pretty smoothly, even though the snow cover turned out to be thin and soft. When it got too soft, I wiped the snow from the rock to find a grip underneath. I had to be careful where I put my feet. It was different from lower down, where I always found a good place for my feet in firm snow and ice. Around noon some clouds moved in, reducing visibility at times, but they offered a welcome break from the scorching sun that had been beating down all morning. In the clouds it was gray and bright at the same time. I climbed to almost 6600 meters. The incline of the upper part of the wall up to the rock band looked about 50 to 60 degrees on snow and ice and appeared relatively easy. It seemed that we ought to be able to climb the 2000 meters from advanced base camp to the rock band in a single day. This would get us pretty high already, leaving another 1000 meters to the summit. This was doable!

Feeling happy with my reconnaissance, I turned back. Fortunately I could down-climb the steeper sections. Placing an anchor for a rappel would have been challenging: The layers in the rock were not optimal and the warm sunlight had made the ice too soft to place a screw.

When I returned Don was inside the tent. We spent another night at 6100 meters, and Don was more comfortable than on the first night. The following morning he felt fine, but the weather had turned bad, and we decided to descend to base camp. Having spent two nights at this altitude was already pretty good. I had reached 6600 meters, which meant that I should now be pretty well acclimatized. In fact, I was probably acclimatized enough to attempt the summit. On Everest in the spring I had climbed up the West Shoulder to 7500 meters after five nights at Base Camp and one night at 6400 meters. Now I had already spent more nights up high than in the spring. This thought was comforting since it made me realize that we could actually start for the summit with the next weather window.

We left the tent, the remaining food, and the rope at a well-protected depot, which we anchored solidly to make sure we would not lose our gear in the next big storm. Going down was easy. We ate some food at advanced base camp and then carried on to base camp. Now we could enjoy full dining service again! The weather worsened, and it started to rain. Perfect timing. We were back down, and it was my birthday.

Frenchmen Yannick Graziani and Stéphane Benoist were also back at base camp. We had run into them in Kathmandu, and I had known both Yannick and Stéphane for quite some time. They had decided pretty late in the season to also attempt the South Face of Annapurna. We wanted to share a permit, but this was far too spontaneous for the Nepalese authorities. They would not have conceded even if we had offered to pay them, but this did not stop the pair from coming, and I was happy to see them. They followed a different acclimatization rotation since they did not have a permit for Annapurna. They had spent a few days in a side valley and climbed to 6000 meters from there. Now they wanted to rest and sit out the bad weather. We could have teamed up with them, but they were not sure which route they were going to tackle. Stéphane wanted to attempt a new route to the central summit, while Yannick wanted to be more spontaneous and flexible. I had the feeling, though, that he had a pretty good idea of what he wanted to climb.

The weather was miserable, but it did not worry me in the slightest. It was probably good to rest for a few days. I had been on the move nonstop since our arrival. For my birthday we went out for dinner, walking over to the lodge. Yannick ordered a huge amount of food, and I was surprised in the end that everything got eaten. This fine feast was crowned with a piece of Kaji's birthday cake, and after watching an episode of *Game of Thrones* on the computer we all fell into a deep and happy sleep.

Two days later, on October 6, Yannick, Stéphane, and I went back to our advanced base camp. Don decided to catch up with us later since he did not want to walk in the rain and preferred to wait for the weather to clear. As it had snowed higher up, we decided to stay at advanced base camp for another day and see how the face would react to the fresh snow. The following day was beautiful. The sun was beating down, which gave the fresh snow the chance to either settle or slide down the face. It felt almost excruciatingly hot, and we were basking in the sun in our T-shirts at 5000 meters. It was almost impossible to get away from the heat. It was boiling inside the tent and unbearably bright outside. The sun was working hard to clear the snow from the face, and huge avalanches started to thunder down it. The wind was also working hard: we could see huge plumes of snow coming off the ridges. The face was getting a spring cleaning in the fall, with the wind sweeping off everything that was not glued to the rock.

Our weather report from Meteotest in Switzerland forecast brilliant weather for the following three days. We double-checked with Yannick and Stéphane, who received their weather reports from Yannick Giezendanner in Chamonix, and they agreed. Don and I wanted to see how high we would get on the face and thought that if things were going smoothly we might even attempt the summit. I had thought about it carefully, with all day to ponder it. On Everest in the spring I had climbed up to 7500 meters on the sixth day of the expedition. We had now been on Annapurna for eighteen days. I was convinced that we could make it in three days. With our acclimatization, I thought, we ought to be able to reach 6900 meters on the first day, and from there it ought to be possible to get to the summit and back in two days.

This, however, required us to climb more or less without a rope and without any safety gear up to 6900 meters. The route to the rock band was not that steep, maybe less than I'd judged earlier, mostly ice at about 45 to 55 degrees, intercepted by some steeper sections of about 70 to 80 degrees. Such an incline did not necessarily require a rope. We could rope up and put in protection on the steep section beyond the first high camp, which I had already climbed. The good thing was that we were not under pressure. We'd see how we would get on. If it did not work out, we would at least be well acclimatized for our next attempt. I was also aware that my threshold for climbing without a rope was higher than Don's. I had to be careful not to expect the same from him as I did from myself. It could be dangerous to put him under such pressure.

On October 8, early in the morning, Don and I headed for the South Face. Dan, who was in charge of taking photos, and Jonah, who was filming, joined us. The ascent to the bergschrund took a while since Dan and Jonah were not as well acclimatized as Don and I.

The weather was fine, but the wind had not abated. I was confident that everything was in place. I had never seen such perfect conditions on this mountain. Finally we had the chance to give it a proper go. I felt very optimistic and extremely motivated. Don, on the other hand, seemed tense. Once we had reached the bergschrund, Don told me out of the blue that he had decided not to continue. His gut feeling was that the terrain was technically too demanding for him to climb without a rope. His words sounded final and left no doubt about his decision. Even if I had been able to convince him to come along, it would not have been good. There was nothing to discuss, though. He was not coming, and that was it!

At first Don's decision triggered a feeling of frustration in me. In my world, everything was perfect: the weather, the conditions, everything. Why didn't he want to continue? But it quickly became clear to me that the terrain higher up looked different to his eyes than mine. I had to accept it. In my view, climbing this route required moving without a rope to the rock band. From there we would have roped up anyway to get over the headwall. Since I had climbed to 6600 meters, I was convinced that this section could be climbed without a rope. Don and I had discussed this at base camp, and he had agreed. Had we roped up on this terrain, it would have taken us ages to get to the bottom of the headwall. We would have been exhausted by the time the real technical climbing started. Additionally, the extra nights up high would have had a negative effect on our bodies. Between 6500 and 7000 meters, even bivouacking sucks the energy out of you.

Although I had climbed with Don before, I had probably overestimated his willingness to climb a technical route without a rope. We had never done a real technical climb together. Because Don had been on Annapurna before, I had assumed that he would be able to gauge the intricacies of the South Face and that he would be confident enough to climb it. After all, he had agreed to come. I guess I must have been naïve and expected him to climb at my level. On the other hand, I really appreciated Don's honesty and the fact that he put a stop to his expedition before he got into trouble. It was right that he had heeded his gut feeling and hadn't put himself into a situation he was unable to handle just to please me. Such an expedition was mentally demanding. It was important for teammates to support each other with positive thoughts and not get each other down by thinking negatively.

▲ ▲ ▲

But what was I supposed to do now? Carry on alone? Or join the others and go down? I had not been prepared for such a situation, even though I had soloed the face before. On this day I had expected to climb as a team. I was still hanging on to the thought that our plan could work and that we still had a good chance to reach the summit together. Thinking about routes I had soloed before, the psychological threshold of at least having a look at the face was not that high. "I am going to have a look," I said to Don, Dan, and Jonah. I was totally aware that I had to set off immediately, that otherwise it would have been difficult to let them go. I knew myself well, and I knew that I had to say good-bye. I had to follow my own path and forget everything around me. I had experienced this on my other solo climbs. If I did not manage to step into my own world, it would not work. I would sit at base camp in brilliant weather and be annoyed with myself that I was not somewhere on the mountain. Letting such precious days go by without achieving anything in the Himalaya is a luxury that a mountaineer like me cannot afford.

I did not get into a discussion with the others. There were gazillions of reasons for not soloing the South Face of Annapurna. I had fallen here before, and I had been lucky to survive. But this was not the moment to question myself and my abilities. I had to decide for myself what I wanted to do. I wanted to make the most of this beautiful day and go climbing, no matter where and how high. I wanted to climb, not sit around, and so I followed my heart.

When I crossed the bergschrund, I had no idea how I would proceed. Several scenarios buzzed around in my head. One was to spend three days on the face and get better acclimatized and then maybe join Yannick and Stéphane. At the time, they were still intending to tackle the Japanese pillar, and since they were good friends of mine I was sure they would let me tag along. Or maybe Don would change his mind and decide to give it a go in these perfect conditions after all. Maybe he had only slept badly and was too nervous. I did not want to put any pressure on myself, and I consciously started to relax.

After I had climbed for about an hour, I knew that I would not stay at Camp 1 at 6100 meters. The weather was far too good and the conditions too ideal to spend the day in a tiny tent. I would continue but leave there all the gear I had taken for Don and me for three days. My plan was to carry only a light pack and climb as high as possible. I could also climb the snowy and icy sections during the night, which would keep me moving when it was cold and save me carrying heavy gear, such as a sleeping bag and warm clothing. With this tactic, I would rest during the day, when it was sunny and warm. In the worst-case scenario, I would have to descend if I got stuck on terrain that was too technical. Leaving the provisions at Camp 1 gave me a backup, as I could always come back here and find food, propane, and a sleeping bag. All of a sudden it was clear to me: I had to go and have a look at what was possible.

At the beginning it is never easy to put your mind to soloing, especially when you have not been prepared for it. I usually plan everything meticulously prior to an expedition. I know every move and what I need to do. On Annapurna, however, I was not quite sure whether I was carrying the right gear. It all happened a bit too quickly, and I did not have the opportunity to think everything through carefully. I was forced to rely on my long years of experience. The pristine conditions helped me to quickly concentrate on the climbing.

It was distinctly colder than it had been the last time I had been here. According to the weather forecast, the wind would remain strong for the rest of the day and abate during the night. The following day was forecast to be calm, and three dry days were predicted. Clouds would gather by day, with no precipitation. Wetter weather was supposed to move in afterward. It was still too early to be more precise, but the forecast showed no storm brewing. The only worry left was the strong wind still blowing on the summit.

It was not far to Camp 1, where Don and I had left a stove, some food and propane, and a rope. I put the tent and stove into my backpack. Even though I was planning to keep moving all the time, I wanted to have the tent in case I had to sit out the wind somewhere. I left the rope behind since I had taken a 6-millimeter cord from advanced base camp. Wanting to save weight, I did not take my sleeping bag and tied it to an anchor together with the remaining gas, food, and the rope. I emptied my pack of everything that was not needed for climbing. I packed my down jacket for the night, but otherwise I was pretty economical with my clothing. I wore only a stretch overall, a pair of hard-shell pants, a fleece hoodie, and a thin PrimaLoft jacket. I carried one pair of double-layered gloves for climbing and one pair of thick down mittens. I even removed the hip belt and the carrier system of the backpack. Every gram counted.

After having repacked everything, my backpack was almost empty, and the difference was remarkable. I had reduced the weight from about fourteen pounds, which was already pretty light, to seven or eight pounds. It felt good.

The steep section beyond Camp 1 was covered in a lot more snow than when I had come here during my acclimatization rotation. Then the rock was bare, but now everything was covered in a frozen layer of snow, and the sunlight was not strong enough to soften it. I had no trouble getting up it, and I was convinced that down-climbing this section would not be a problem in these conditions.

The ascent was magical, almost surreal. A climber could not have wished for better conditions, but I restrained myself and moved at a moderate pace to avoid overdoing it. Once muscles accumulate lactic acid up here, the body isn't able to get rid of it, and above 7000 meters that slows you down significantly. I had to save my strength since I wanted to climb through the night or at least until the sun was on the face again. I was prepared to climb nonstop for twenty-four hours.

I was oblivious to my surroundings. Climbing was the only thing that mattered. I was in my own little world: there was nothing but the mountain and me. I lived for the moment and dug my ice axe deeply into the solid snow. It stuck, which gave me confidence. When I thrust my right axe into the snow, it hit hard ground. Using less force, I tried again a bit farther to the right, where the snow was firmer. It was safe. I let my feet follow and swung the axe again. This was my world. These were my thoughts, my actions. Ice axes and crampons were the only things on my mind.

The ascent up to the headwall turned out to be pretty straightforward. The slope had an incline of about 40 to 50 degrees, which allowed me to walk on all fours. I felt comfortable on such terrain. Most of the time I was relying on my crampons and using my ice axes only as support. Up to about 6600 meters, wind and the occasional spindrift were my only companions. These small snow avalanches triggered by the wind are usually pretty harmless, but if they carry too much snow they can throw a climber off balance.

I climbed to just below the headwall at 7000 meters, where I wanted to pitch my tent and wait for the wind to abate. If it did, I would continue. If it did not, I would descend. The thought of spending a night in a tent without a sleeping bag was horrible—that was not what I had planned for.

Just below the rock band I found a spot that at first seemed suitable for my purpose. I didn't need much space but wanted to be able to sit. Suddenly I spotted a small pillar above me on the right. Being in quite a protected spot, it looked like a good place to wait without exposing myself to possible avalanches. I climbed about 100 meters to get closer to the top of the pillar, which involved negotiating a rocky section. Nothing very difficult, just necessary in order to get back into the snow. When I reached the head of the pillar, I realized that it was far from suitable for pitching my tent: It was sloping and covered in ice. I tried to chop out a ledge, but it was hopeless. After having scraped off about 10 centimeters of hard snow, I hit thick blue ice, which meant that I would not be able to build a platform in reasonable time. Hoping to find a better campsite lower down, I descended. This situation was disheartening. Was this already the end of my jaunt? Did I have to go back to Camp 1? The wind was still howling higher up, and it was too dangerous to continue.

Before I started my descent I wanted to take a photo of the rock band. I had never been so high on the face before, and from here I got a good look at the headwall. As I stood slightly to the side of the route, I could see the structure and the profile of the face much better than I would have from up closer. A photo of the wall would make it easier to find it again in the dark.

I thrust my two ice axes deeply into the hard snow. With my crampons I tried to flatten the ground some to stand more comfortably. Balancing at about 1500 meters above the bergschrund, I took off my mitten and hung it carefully over one of my axes. The camera was attached to my harness, but its cord was too short to allow me to take a photo. I unhooked it from the loop and pressed the shutter button. To be on the safe side, I wanted to take a second photo, but before I had a chance to press the shutter button again, I was hit by something coming from above. I immediately grabbed my ice axes, waited, and hoped that it would be over soon. Snow was crashing down on me: I was being attacked by a huge spindrift. I could feel the pressure build between the rock face and my body, and I was struggling to keep my balance. Finally the pressure eased. I was prepared for more, my whole body shaking in anticipation, but nothing else happened.

That was a close call! But it was over now; the snow had stopped pouring down on me. Both my mitten and my camera had disappeared into the abyss. I was annoyed and relieved at the same time. I was still on the face but had escaped a fall by a whisker. I wanted to get away as quickly as possible. The next mega-spindrift could hit me at any time.

I was now left with one down mitten and my two-layered climbing gloves. This could be a problem. Again I wondered whether the time had come to go down. Had Don's intuition been good? But I had been climbing without my down mittens all day and had only just put them on. It ought to be possible for me to continue without them. The terrain was getting steeper, and I had brought my gloves especially for the headwall. If it got too cold I would have to descend, but for the time being I could continue. The mitten would have just been an excuse. I stayed calm and tried to analyze the situation. Now that I did not have a camera, I did not have a good picture of the route, but that was not really decisive either. I had only one down mitten left, but I had not fallen. Now I had to act immediately to find a protected spot.

Before I descended I took the time to have another look at the face. From my position the conditions looked perfect. I could see a white line winding its way through the snow-covered rock. I had not seen this in 2007 or in 2008, but that had been in spring. I wondered whether the snow up there was hard or soft. The fact that the wind had been blowing hard for a few days gave me confidence since it would have blown off any snow that had not been solidly frozen to the rock. In order to find out whether I could follow that line of ice and snow, I needed to climb higher to take stock.

At this moment I realized how much risk I was prepared to take and how high I had already climbed up on the face. It did not really matter now whether I carried on or turned back. I had accepted the risk. It occurred to me that I might not come back from the face. Suddenly there was no longer an afterward. The spindrift had flicked a switch inside me, and I was now prepared to give everything.

This attitude was selfish, but at the time and place it was fine for me. I did not need to discuss this with anyone. I did what felt right for me and did not have to justify my actions. I was prepared to take the risk, no matter what happened. It was just Annapurna and me. The rules were clear. I had no fear, and I did not mind being exposed in the middle of the face. I could neither win nor lose. No matter what happened, I had accepted the situation.

I climbed down the pillar, hoping I would find a suitable spot to wait for the wind to die down. I was no longer worried about the spindrift but was now completely focused again on my ice axes and crampons. I needed to feel whether my crampons could find a good grip underneath me. When I reached the short rocky section, I carefully lowered my right foot and put it on a small ledge. I started putting weight onto my front points and slowly put all of my weight onto this foot. I stretched my arms out and put my left foot next to my right. I let my ice axes follow the movement and brought them down to shoulder height. I placed the two blades on top of a small ledge and consciously pulled down on them. Then I stretched my arms again, and again lowered one foot after the other. This footstep was a bit bigger. All the front points of my crampons were on the rock. I put weight on them again and moved the ice axes down. Five such moves took me back to the snow, where I could walk upright with my axes and climb down step by step more easily.

A hundred meters below I found a crevasse, which turned out to be the perfect bivouac spot. I was able to pitch my tent inside it and was protected from the wind and spindrifts. I felt annoyed that I had not seen the crevasse during my ascent. It would have saved me a lot of hassle! I had climbed up right beside it without noticing it, but it had been completely covered in snow. When climbing down, having nearly fallen into it, I felt like a blind hen finding a grain of corn. Now it was time to eat and drink as much water as possible, since I wanted to head out again as soon as the wind died down. Once the snow had melted, I drank the tepid water without waiting for it to boil. I managed to drink about one and a half liters in no time and was even able to fill my water bottle. A piece of cheese Don had given me at the base of the wall was a welcome change from the sweet energy bars I usually eat. It was cheddar, and being Swiss I am sure it tastes delicious only at 7000 meters.

The moment the sun disappeared from the face, the wind also calmed. We had observed the same phenomenon at advanced base camp the previous evening, and Stéphane had experienced it on Annapurna during an earlier attempt.

He had explained to me that on some days the sun created a strong thermal that died down as soon as the face was in the shade. I had frequently felt upwind that day. It was extremely likely that wind and a thermal would come back once the sun hit the face in the morning. This meant the only way to the summit was to climb during the night, just like Swiss mountaineers Erhard Loretan and Jean Troillet had done in 1986 when they climbed up and down the North Face of Everest in forty-three hours.

I had two choices: up or down. Staying here in a bivouac with my limited gear was out of the question. I had only been here a very short time, but I was already getting cold and needed to move again. This could be the chance of a lifetime, and it needed 100 percent commitment. I was optimistic and rational at the same time, which was decisive. Such undertakings do not allow emotions. The only thing that works is to rationally focus on your actions. As soon as you allow your emotions to get in the way, you lose your nerve. And for one stricken by panic in this hostile environment, each step could be the last.

I started giving myself orders. I told myself that it was too early to give up. From earlier solo climbs I had found it useful to give myself commands. This let me believe that I was not making decisions for myself but for somebody else. I looked at myself from the outside and observed myself climbing. This person did the right thing, just like I told him to do.

So, up we go! The break had not been long. I left the tent and started out very slowly. Moving—plus the hot water bottle in my pocket—brought warmth back into my body. I had left everything at the bivouac: backpack, tent, and stove. I was only carrying the cord, which I had tied around my back, my water bottle, and a few bars of chocolate. I would climb as high as possible and would then descend to Camp 1. I allowed myself that freedom and did not put myself under pressure. This was my usual approach. When I felt that it was time to turn around, I did, no matter for what reason.

I was completely detached from the world below. There was nothing but climbing. No goal, no future, no past. I was climbing in the here and now. One swing of the ice axe after the other, one step after the other. I saw only my ice axes and how they penetrated the snow and ice. My view narrowed. There I was in the middle of this gigantic face with very limited equipment. I felt light but also extremely exposed. I knew that the tiniest mistake would mean certain death. However, I was not scared about making a mistake. I was still giving myself orders. I was controlling the person climbing the South Face of Annapurna. It was not me. If this person fell, it would not really be me.

The uninterrupted line of ice and snow crossing the rock band in combination with the light of my headlamp made it possible for me to find the way in the dark. I liked climbing at night. It made me concentrate. Only the next step counted. It could be the last, but I did not mind. I was not worried about routefinding or about not being able to climb the next section. I was living for the moment, and right now everything was fine: Conditions were perfect. Rock and ice were covered in hard snow, just like on the Eiger North Face in perfect winter conditions. Whenever possible, I switched off my headlamp to save battery power, although it should have had enough charge to last the whole night. I knew cold temperatures can sap battery power in no time.

I was climbing pretty far to the right. The lower part had a few steep, icy sections, but it was not hard blue ice. The ice was covered in a sheet of hard snow, and wherever the ice was uncovered it did not chip. I used my one-hit approach, aimed at hitting each axe blow just once, precisely. This increased my speed but required total concentration. As I pulled I had to consciously avoid moving the axe since the tip of the blade sometimes did not sink very deeply into the ice.

It was ideal terrain for a solo climb. As long as I could continue like this, I would be extremely efficient. At 7000 meters the air starts getting thin. This is where the so-called death zone begins, but one can still move around quite freely. I felt light and agile. I didn't have a backpack and wore light clothing. Only the cold bothered me. I was worried about my hands.

The rock next to the ice was well structured. For a short section just below the snow band, the ice line got pretty narrow and steep—about 85 degrees. It was classic alpine ice climbing terrain, just like in Chamonix. The ice section ended just below vertical rock. Here I was able to move onto a small ramp on the right, where the ice line was even narrower but not too steep at about 70 degrees. I put my right crampon on a rocky ledge in order to move my center of gravity. I then moved my left ice axe to the right and found myself again in a perpendicular position. From here the ice track widened again slowly. The ice was smoother and more compact than lower down, where it was a lot more corroded, like hard snow.

A ramp led from the snowfield to the right, and I followed it. I reached another snowfield, where I climbed back toward the left and continued until the route went up more directly over a steep section. From what I had seen from below, I knew that I had to keep to the left and must not get too high. I found a traverse, which led me across to the left. And from here, I thought, the route ought to be clear. The hard snow cover was pretty thin in places, which made me aware of time. I had to be back here before the sun had a chance to soften this layer. Coming back here too late would be fatal, since down-climbing this section in soft snow would be impossible.

I was still making good progress. It was absolutely quiet, and I only heard my own movements, the crampons, the ice axes, and my breathing.

The headwall turned out to be shorter than I had anticipated. As I was not using a rope, it was difficult to say how many pitches it would have been. In the upper section I encountered classic North Face terrain: rocky, with a hard snow cover, and a lot flatter than lower down. I could immediately feel the change of the incline, as I could put most of my weight on my feet. I kept to the left for quite a while before I climbed straight up and then moved over to the right toward the snowy patch. From here the terrain got steeper and the snow cover thinner, so that I sometimes hit rock with my ice axe. Even though this was my favorite terrain, I could not get rid of the feeling that I had to work hard before I was rewarded with flatter terrain. My calves were burning. The route seemed endless. I had to be there soon! Finally the terrain got flatter. I had reached the end of the headwall, and the snow felt more compact here. I immediately felt less exposed. Above me in the dark there was a big white snowfield.

It was only here that it became clear to me where I was and what that meant. For a moment I allowed my thoughts to wander. I knew that from now on it would be a race against the sun and the wind. I could not afford to turn back too late. If the sun softened the layer of hard snow and ice, it would be my end. However, it was still early, and turning around for this reason would have been just an excuse. I did not check my watch, since this would have worried me. So far, I could see no light on the horizon. As the terrain was not too difficult, I could easily continue until dawn. I hoped the thermal winds would not be too strong in the morning.

My position was beginning to worry me. I was very high, very exposed, and I would have to down-climb with no gear whatsoever. Rappelling with a 60-meter rope, five bolts, and one ice screw was unrealistic. I switched to survival mode. For a brief moment, I was indecisive. I would have loved to turn back, but I kept on telling myself: "Keep on climbing." The weather would hold. I had come so far, and now it would not really make a difference.

I ordered myself: "Continue!"

I calmed down a bit as I climbed. I had switched off my headlamp, and the sound of the crunching snow was somehow comforting. My right hand was getting cold, and I put the down mitten on, even though it was the wrong hand. It warmed up pretty quickly. I concentrated hard and found my rhythm again. Everything sorted itself out, and the thoughts disturbing my flow had disappeared. I was back in tune with my movements, blow by blow, step by step. The snow slope seemed endless, but up here it was not so steep anymore.

I crossed another steep rocky band before I reached flatter ground covered in hard snow. Here I stopped briefly to change the down mitten from my right hand to my left, and then I veered left. The terrain got steeper again. I climbed through a gully toward the black sky. Once again it felt steep. Was I too far to the left? Should I have kept more to the right? Even though I had an inkling that the terrain would have been better on the right, I continued through the steep gully to the summit ridge. This may not have been the best route, but it got me there. The last few meters were pretty exhausting.

Suddenly I was standing in the dark below a sky full of stars. The ridge ahead of me went down a ways. I followed it. It went up again and a little later down again. Everything seemed pretty flat up here. Finally I reached a third elevation. Was this the highest point? I could not see any higher point in front of me. The summit was obviously just a prominent point on the ridge, nothing spectacular. With my headlamp switched off I could see the ridge and the surroundings a bit better. The ridge led down until it got lost in the black night. Up here it was significantly colder and windier. As soon as I stopped I started to get cold. I had to move again.

Suddenly I felt that I had to go back down as quickly as possible. I did not feel triumphant or victorious about having reached the summit. I felt uncomfortable, nervous, and scared. I wanted to get away. I suddenly longed for the bergschrund. It was 1:00 a.m. I immediately started my descent. Would I be able to get down? After a short while, I stopped. It was difficult to see my tracks, but it was crucial not to lose them. In the hard snow and ice I could sometimes only make out the little dots made by my crampons. At first, higher up, I could descend facing forward, which was easier. As soon as I was in the gully, I climbed down backward following the traces of my ice axes. I hardly ever looked down. Whenever I lost my tracks, I stopped, looked left and right, and usually found my tracks about a meter next to me.

Lower down, where I had traversed to the left, I was able to climb down again facing forward, but once I had reached the small rock band I had to climb backward. As far as I could remember it was pretty straight down from here. I felt under control. It was certainly not the first time that I was down-climbing on difficult ground, but I still wanted to get down as quickly as possible. I expected to be able to down-climb most sections, but I knew exactly which sections I would have to rappel.

From the upper edge of the snowfield the terrain got steeper again. The snow cover was pretty thin here, and

I had to do my first rappel of 30 meters on an Abalakov V-thread. I then down-climbed a few meters before setting up the next V-thread. For this I drilled two holes that interconnected at the end to form a V-like channel in the ice and threaded my rope through the channel. After three rappels combined with some down-climbing, I was back at the traverse, where I could down-climb without any problems. It all went pretty smoothly; I had found my rhythm again. The consistency of the hard snow was still ideal, and my ice axes had a good grip.

The headwall required eight rappels on V-threads. The other sections I could down-climb facing inward. In order to find hard blue ice for my V-threads, I had to move on pretty uncomfortable and steep ground. As I always used the entire rope length for my rappels, I made a knot at the end of the rope to prevent me from slipping off. I then switched into down-climbing mode again and slowly pulled the rope down. Once it had fallen down, I simply let it dangle and continued to climb. The knot in the rope was attached to my descender, which was a good way to prevent my losing it.

This rappelling technique felt right, and my tracks were pointing me in the right direction. I knew exactly what to expect. I did not have to worry about coming to a dead end. I just had to follow the little tracks. This ought to have been comforting, but I felt extremely tense. I tried to concentrate and focus, and I kept on telling myself that everything would be all right. I had again lost sense of time and just kept on climbing. I began feeling tired, and I had to force myself to thrust my crampons firmly into the hard snow. I was using my front points most of the time and swinging my ice axes into the ice with less force than before. They probably would have just pulled out had my feet slipped! At about 4:00 a.m. I reached my bivouac at the base of the headwall. I crawled into the crevasse and without even unstrapping my crampons, fell into my tent. Given the circumstances, I did not care if I ripped holes in the fabric. I melted snow and drank. I knew that it shouldn't take me very long to get down from here, but I still filled my bottle with water. I had already done the steepest sections of the climb. Day would break soon, and then I would be able to see properly again. While I was putting everything into my backpack, I felt something hard in the outer pocket. Maybe something to eat that I had forgotten about? No, it was my satellite phone. I had been sure that I had left it in the camp at 6100 meters. I continued to pack, and for the first time I thought about down below, the future, and things other than just climbing. There was another world out there. It was a tricky moment. My emotions set in, and I no longer wanted to be up there. I wanted to get down as quickly as possible. But first I wrote a text message to Don. Had the others been worried about me? I had only been thinking about myself the whole time. I almost made a big mistake and let my emotions surge. I pulled myself together and consciously suppressed them. They could be fatal in situations like this. But the cat was out of the bag, and all of a sudden I was scared of falling and dying. Until that moment I had suppressed this. Fear had emerged only on very few occasions. But now the world had changed. I could see a future again.

When I got back on my feet, my calves were as hard as rock, with occasional stabbing pain shooting through them. But I was able to concentrate again, knowing very well that every step could be my last. I was still in the middle of the South Face of Annapurna. Dawn was slowly breaking toward the east, and I was hoping that the wind would not immediately pick up again. I was absorbed in trying to feel my feet with every step. Since I could not see them, I had to sense whether I had put them in the right place or not. The ice axes were only there for support. I was relying

100 percent on my feet. Now I had reentered the world of the mountain and me, and I was focused on every single step. I registered every sound and was as tense as a spring. If I slipped or another mini avalanche came down on me, I would have to react immediately. Everything around me was still frozen hard.

After having negotiated the last steep section, I could finally turn around and face down. What a relief! I down-climbed a rib that led to our depot camp. Apathetically I packed all the gear I had left there and carried on. My pack was now significantly heavier. For a split second I thought of simply throwing it down the mountain. At that moment the pack was a burden, and I just wanted to get rid of the heavy load on my back. I felt relieved when I reached the bergschrund and found the thin cord I had fixed to the rocky ledge with which to rappel. This was the door leading me back into the real world.

Finally I was off the face. I let my eyes wander across the glacier to see whether my friends were coming up. They must have seen me descending. But I couldn't see anybody, and I just kept on walking. It felt like being in a movie that keeps on running even after everyone stops watching it. Everything seemed to happen automatically. I wasn't in pain, and I barely noticed anything apart from the fact that my vision was blurred. Sweat was running into my eyes.

I traversed the glacier toward the moraine on the right. When I came around a corner, suddenly Tenji was in front of me, just like that. Out of the blue. I was so happy to see him!

We looked at each other.

"Summit?" he asked.

"Yes, summit," I responded.

That was all I could say. I was in a different world again, and Tenji seemed like an angel. If anything went wrong now, there would be someone to help me. It was no longer my sole responsibility. Tenji opened his bag and retrieved a

Coke and an apple. When we climbed Everest together in 2012, I had carried a liter and a half of Coke up to the South Col. On summit day, we lived off Coke. He had remembered that as well as the fact that I could eat tons of apples.

We didn't talk much. I had nothing to say. I was still in a trance, and everything seemed to bounce off me.

Soon afterward, Don, Dan, and Janine arrived. They congratulated me and took pictures of me. Life carried on.

My apathy turned into nervousness, however, and I wanted to get away as quickly as possible. I felt scared. There were all these people around me, and I did not know what to tell them. I knew them, but at the same time they seemed like strangers. My eyes were burning from the sweat that was trickling down my forehead.

It had been twenty-eight hours since I'd left advanced base camp. I had been completely exposed and left to my own devices. Every single move had needed to be perfect. It was over now, but my body was still full of adrenaline. My head was empty, and I felt like an alien. Everything seemed out of context, and I was just tagging along. We got back to advanced base camp in no time.

▲ ▲ ▲

On October 9 at 9:30 a.m., back at advanced base camp, I called Nicole. There was a moment of silence after I told her that I had climbed the face alone, but at the same time I knew she was relieved that everything had gone well and that I had come back safe and sound. The conversation did not last long. It was always difficult to talk in these moments. Back home Nicole was in a completely different world and was busy with her job. We needed to be patient and wait for me to get home to talk properly. We were both used to the distance that gets between us during such an expedition. It was almost routine. Even though I was dead tired and my legs felt like jelly, I wanted to descend to base camp that day. I knew I would even feel more exhausted the next day. My head was spinning, and all I wanted was peace and quiet. The descent was a question of willpower. Crossing the moraine was draining. I was so drained of energy that I had to stop a few times during the 50-meter ascent from the moraine up to base camp.

I could hardly sleep that night. My head buzzed with random thoughts about climbing, rappelling, spindrifts, and the like. One minute I was climbing up, the next I was climbing down. One time I was able to climb a particular section, the next time I was not and fell. Such scenes kept recurring the whole night. As soon as it got light, I could not wait to get out of the tent. I was still alive! I needed a change of scenery and had to do something to distract myself. I wanted to leave base camp, and for that matter Nepal, as quickly as possible. I hoped that the tension would ease once I was home and with Nicole.

The mountain continued to haunt me the following nights. The abyss, the emptiness, the cold, the wind, and the spindrifts. Annapurna seemed to consume me completely. Night after night, I fell. In my dreams I lost control over my climbing, and this got worse with every night. I would fall off the face and see my body lying at the base of the mountain. At times I wore the same green helmet I had worn in 2007, when I was hit by a rock. The nights became one single nightmare. What I had experienced up there must have just been too intense— the twenty-eight hours of full concentration, of knowing that a single mistake would mean death. I might not have exceeded my physical limits, but I must have gone past my psychological ones.

I was still in my own world, although I was no longer as focused as I had been. I had no idea what to tell my friends about my experience up there, and I did not really feel the need to do so. I was alone with my thoughts and would not have been able to express them properly. Suddenly everything seemed gloomy, and I had this uncertain fear that something bad might happen. Home became my focus and the solution to my problems. I was convinced that everything would be all right once I got back to Switzerland. I left Nepal as soon as possible.

Despite my rushed departure I had an amazing time with all the friends who were with me on this Annapurna expedition, especially Don, who motivated me to attempt the face solo. Just before my departure I gave him one of my ice axes as a memento. I wanted to dedicate the route to the two climbers who had been the first to attempt it: Jean-Christophe Lafaille and Pierre Béghin. The route had been their vision, and I had just realized what they had conceived. The fact that I had climbed the line I had been dreaming about for many years became a sort of liberation for me.

Both Béghin and Lafaille lost their lives in the Himalaya. They are only two of many examples that reflect the fine line between life and death in the mountains. Erhard Loretan, who fell to his death while guiding in the Alps, is another one of these examples. He was the one who taught me what was possible in the high Himalaya without taking too much gear. Yes, I had trained hard for my expedition to Annapurna, and I had planned it meticulously. But training and planning alone had not been decisive for my success. I had also had a good portion of luck. I was fortunate to have had such perfect conditions and that the spindrift did not throw me off balance and down into the abyss. I had been extremely exposed. It had seemed normal at the time. I had decided what was right for me, and I had simply functioned. During the climb it had been perfectly all right for me to accept such high risks. I had put all my eggs into one basket. Climbing such walls demands willingness to take risks.

Maybe the events on Everest were part of the reason I had been prepared to take so much risk. What had happened in the spring that year had shaken me pretty badly. It had made me lose my belief in humanity. Those events certainly threw me back into my own world, and afterward I had just wanted to climb—nothing else mattered. I wanted to train and push my body's limits. That was my goal for the summer of 2013. I wanted to live, and maybe I wanted to live feeling that I had nothing to lose.

The events of the night on the South Face of Annapurna had left their mark on me. There were many unforgettable moments. Stepping onto the ridge after having climbed the headwall was one such moment and feeling totally liberated when I finally tied into the fixed rope to rappel across the bergschrund was another. Some of my decisions were made by following my gut feeling. I cannot really explain why I sometimes decided to climb on the left or on the right. I simply followed my intuition, which is the result of years of climbing experience. I recognized myself in the Italian mountaineer Walter Bonatti, who wrote after his solo climb of the West Face of the Petit Dru: "For the next five days it was like living in another world; like entering an unknown dimension; like being in a mystical visionary state in which the impossible did not exist and anything could happen." I felt much the same way on Annapurna. Somehow everything seemed possible. Everything was in reach, and everything worked out.

▲ ▲ ▲

When I finally got home after the expedition and was back in my familiar surroundings, things did not get back to normal as I had hoped. I realized that when I was climbing the face, I had actually finished with my life. This realization shook me completely. In hindsight, I simply did not understand how I could possibly have been prepared to take so much risk. I had accepted putting my life on the line. On the South Face of Annapurna, this feeling gave me a lot of strength and willpower, but now it was giving me a lot of grief. I struggled to get along in everyday life.

During the climb it felt good to be so uncompromising. There was no afterward, and there was no worry, no fear, because there was no future. There was only the here and now. At home I started questioning my actions. I returned home with a mountaineering trophy, but had I been doing the right thing? How did I end up being in this trance-like state? What about Nicole and my family? I had a responsibility toward them.

A few days after I returned to the Bernese Oberland, Nicole left for a climbing holiday in Turkey. She had planned this trip thinking that I would still be in Nepal during this time. Being left on my own, I felt my world was crumbling. My nightmares continued, and I was still falling to my death on the South Face of Annapurna, night after night. Now the events on Everest also came back to haunt me. I had started taking sleeping pills, but I still woke up drenched in sweat because there was someone at the end of my bed wanting to crush my skull. I was scared of falling asleep and wanted to stay awake to fend off possible attackers. During the day I was so tired that I hardly managed to go for an hour's run. I was suffering from panic attacks, and my life was out of control for many months.

In previous years I had repeatedly gotten myself into highly stressful situations in the mountains, but I guess the psychological pressure was just too high this time around. While on Everest, I had experienced fear of death and had lost all faith in humankind, whereas on Annapurna I was looking death in the eye—and I was solely responsible. This had simply been too much for my psyche. I had been living an illusion, convinced that once I had finished my project on the South Face, my life would go on as usual, with self-confidence. But things got worse. I could no longer trust anyone and could not get rid of the feeling that everyone wanted to harm me. It became obvious to me that I had not gotten over the incident with the Sherpas and that I had only pushed it to the back of my mind.

I felt lost. I was unable to share my experience on Annapurna with anyone, even Nicole. I was convinced that nobody who was not a mountaineer doing solo climbs could possibly fathom what I had done and experienced up there. Annapurna had made me lonely, and my fears made me withdraw even more. I then felt ashamed. How could someone so rational as myself fight something so irrational as fear? I had never expected to face a situation where I had such little control over my life.

Finally I came to a dead end. I had mastered the South Face of Annapurna. What else was there left to do? This could not be topped. I was used to making progress, with projects lined up and every single step getting me a bit farther. But now I was stuck. My fire had gone out, and I had lost all motivation. I no longer felt like myself and could barely face giving interviews to the media. This extreme situation was new and unknown territory for me.

It became clear that I would only get out of this dismal state by seeking professional help, which would also involve medication. Otherwise I would just continue going around in circles. Getting out of this spiral of self-doubt and fear was one of the most formative experiences in my life. I found out a lot about myself, and I am still in the process of finding out more. However, I don't wish for anyone to experience something like this. In a way, it felt like training, when you have to push yourself to your limits to get stronger, even though sometimes it is unpleasant. But becoming aware of my own limits has certainly helped me to be more content with my life, to be more confident within myself and with others. In any case, my crisis made me withdraw from public life and concentrate more on my immediate surroundings.

After I had gained some distance, I came to the conclusion that my panic attacks were probably an expression of my fear of myself. I knew exactly how I felt after I had withstood the spindrift: I couldn't have cared less if I had fallen to my death. These thoughts and the recognition that this was probably characteristic of me made me scared of myself. I had no guarantee that I would not take such great risks again. In fact, I was afraid that I would.

I had to get this under control. If I continued like this, it would certainly end in death. But, after all, I was a climber and not someone wanting to commit suicide.

▲ ▲ ▲

But I was not altogether lucky on Annapurna. The fact that the spindrift had hit me at exactly that spot and that I had lost my mitten as well as my camera was actually pretty unlucky. At first the loss of the camera only bothered me because I could not take a good shot of the face. It was only later when I realized that without the camera I would not be able to take a summit photo, which would serve as proof of my successful ascent. But how convincing and informative would a photo have been? A selfie in the dark in the middle of the night? Nevertheless, after my return it did not take long for me to be criticized for not having a summit photo and for having failed to record the route with my GPS watch.

Criticizing me and telling me what I could have done better is easy. If you have never been in such an exposed position in your life, it is almost or completely impossible to understand my decisions. I do not want to sound arrogant, but this is just the way it is. I must have done most things right on Annapurna, otherwise I would not have survived. I had consciously decided not to switch on the tracking mode of my watch to save battery power. To me a GPS is a safety device that is used for navigation in low visibility. I just don't want to risk not having any battery power left in a critical moment. Batteries are pretty sensitive to the cold. In freezing temperatures their performance is only a fraction of what the manufacturers state in their operating instructions. I know from experience that in the cold, the battery power of my model is reduced from fifty to sixteen hours. It took me twenty-eight hours from our advanced base camp to the top and back. And GPS data are not that precise on steep walls anyway. If the horizontal distance is slightly off, even 30 meters could place the summit 200 meters too high or too low. The elevation of Annapurna's summit was clearly too high on my GPS watch.

From the very beginning I was open about the fact that I did not have any proof of having reached the main summit of Annapurna. Since I had climbed during the night and had switched off my headlamp at times to save batteries, I was not visible to my friends at advanced base camp at all times. They also spent a few hours sleeping during the night. The loss of my camera triggered speculation. It didn't take very long for the first doubts to be voiced as to whether I had actually reached the summit. I was even accused of not having climbed the face at all but rather having stayed inside my tent in the crevasse the whole night and having descended the following morning. These accusations came from the mountaineering scene as well as the media.

It is absolutely legitimate to question reports about alpinist achievements, especially when the protagonist is a professional mountaineer and is in the public eye. It seemed to be difficult for the doubters to understand that I was only focused on climbing during the hours on the wall and that I was not thinking about documenting or collecting evidence. The fact that there had not been another mountaineer to have dared such a solo climb made my tales absolutely implausible in the doubters' eyes. My psychological state after the expedition did not help the situation, nor did my not quite hitting the right tone in interviews and not wanting to be in public. I was swamped with interview requests as the media went crazy about the controversy regarding my ascent. I could not, of course, control what was published about it. My withdrawal, on the other hand, led journalists to obtain secondhand information, which they then copied from each other, twisting the story in ways that would confirm their own opinions. It went as far as the assertion that I had paid Tenji and the kitchen boy, Nima Dawa, to testify that they had seen the light of my headlamp just below the summit and that they had watched me descend the following day.

What upset me most was that I was accused of lying. There have been cases in alpine history where mountaineers have not been honest and have come up with their own stories. Mountaineering is different from other sports that are subject to rigid rules and the official keeping of times, heights, and distances, as well as doping controls. Mountaineering, on the other hand, is based on trust. In 1984 the Polish mountaineer Krzysztof Wielicki became the first person to climb an 8000-meter peak in a single day. He scaled Broad Peak in Pakistan and went from base camp to the summit and back in twenty-two hours and ten minutes. In 1993 he climbed the South Face of Shishapangma in Tibet in twenty hours. Krzysztof does not have a single summit photo of his successful ascents of Lhotse and Kangchenjunga, and his photo from the top of Everest could have been taken anywhere. But his reputation as a high-altitude mountaineer is sterling, and so it should be.

Despite technological gizmos, mountaineering achievements will need to continue to be based on trust and climbers' honesty in the future. Solo rock climbs will only be 100 percent verified if they are done on a climbing wall or witnessed from afar by other climbers. Being able to make the decisions for oneself and being responsible for oneself is also part of the beauty of mountaineering.

I tried not to take the accusations personally, but it was not always easy since some came within my wider circle of friends. At the end of the day life would go on, and I had to try not to let the stuff written in the press get me down too much. Yannick Graziani and Stéphane Benoist were two friends who supported my reports. In the end the pair decided to climb my route, and they started the climb on October 16. The conditions they found on the face were not as pristine as when I climbed it a week earlier. A storm had deposited about 60 centimeters of fresh snow onto the face a few days before they started up. This and the fact that they pitched the climb and were sometimes held up by bad weather made them a lot slower: they spent nine days on the face. They followed my route with a few variations, but due to the fresh snow they could not find my tracks, and some used this as "proof" that I had not climbed the face. During their descent Stéphane suffered from severe altitude illness, and it was only thanks to Yannick's selfless deeds that both climbers reached the base of the climb alive. Stéphane got pretty bad frostbite on his fingers. After their climb they both stated publicly that they had no doubt about me being able to climb the face solo in good conditions.

At the beginning of 2014 I was nominated for the Piolet d'Or for my route on Annapurna's South Face. I was very pleased about the nomination, but I spent a lot of time discussing the lack of proof with the organizers. I would have completely understood had they withdrawn the nomination. However, there is no clause in the regulations of the Piolet d'Or that says that proof is needed for a climb. There are numerous examples of great ascents without a summit photo. The nomination was not withdrawn.

In March 2014 I was awarded the Piolet d'Or, as were Raphael Slawinsky and Ian Welsted, who received it for their first ascent of the Northwest Face of K6 in Pakistan. Receiving this public recognition for my climb was definitely good for my self-confidence, even though I figured that it would probably fuel the fire and trigger more criticism. It was interesting to see how the speculations about my climb took on a life of their own in public, especially on the internet, where provocative stories generated more clicks. I had learned my lesson, and I knew that in the future I would have to do a better job documenting my climbs.

I wanted to keep my style though, and not take a photographer along every time I went climbing. Soloing means being alone. A helicopter circling in the background and ready to come to my aid if I got into trouble—that sort of thing makes a big difference. I was interested in the physical challenge of a climb and not in selling adventure or making it into alpine highlight films. The business around mountaineering is rife with staged photo shoots, fake film material, and clever advertising and marketing strategies. There were still plenty of adventures up in the mountains, especially in the Himalaya. How long and how efficiently could a person move at 8000 meters? Has the time come to tackle the Horseshoe, the traverse of Everest, Lhotse, and Nuptse? When will the direct route on the west face of Makalu be climbed? Or the direct route on the north ridge of K2?

I continued to have dreams, but I had to be careful not to let my critics provoke me into feeling that I had to prove something. I knew that I would never go as far as I had gone on the South Face of Annapurna again. It had been too close to the limit. If I did, it would only be a repetition of something I had done before, and it would prove nothing. There was only one way to deal with this situation, and that was by redefining myself and giving my values a new focus.

In order to help me cope with past events, Nicole and I decided to take a sabbatical year and go climbing together in 2014. We needed to spend some quality time with each other. The previous year had not been easy for her. The person she loved had turned out to be self-destructive. We had once agreed that I wouldn't do any more solo climbs, yet I had gone ahead and climbed solo on Annapurna after Don Bowie had backed out. And Annapurna had put a serious strain on our relationship, since I had become a bit of a recluse. Going together on climbing trips and expeditions would give us the opportunity to find each other again and get some peace and quiet together.

SHISHAPANGMA
A STEP TOO FAR

Nicole quit her job so we could go climbing in 2014. We had a lot of time and didn't have much planned for the beginning of the year, apart from some of my professional engagements. Our first destination was Argentina, where we swapped the Swiss winter for the Patagonian summer. After this trip we did a whistle-stop visit to Switzerland and went to the Piolet d'Or award ceremony in Chamonix before we took off again for Spain, where we spent the spring in Siurana. Here we spent our time climbing and getting to know the region while jogging or cycling. When the heat got unbearable in Spain, we continued to France. Céüse was a climbing mecca offering routes for both Nicole and me. In the summer we returned to South America for another four weeks. This time we went to Peru, where we climbed several 6000-meter peaks, including Artesonraju in the Cordillera Blanca.

The distance from home, the withdrawal from public life, and the excursions with Nicole helped me get over the events of the previous year. Even though I had not really digested everything, I no longer suffered from panic attacks and could better see the difference between the events. I had learned that getting over such things is a long process.

The highlight of our trip was planned for the fall. Nicole wanted to find out whether she could climb an 8000-meter peak. The highest point she had reached so far was the 6856-meter Ama Dablam in Nepal, which she had climbed in 2011. She generally coped well with altitude, and she always described our 2009 trip to Gasherbrum II as one of the best trips of her life. The fact that she did not reach the summit due to heavy snowfall did not bother her. She has the technical ability to master such ascents via the normal routes under the right conditions and without carrying too much weight.

She had always wanted to go to Tibet, and so we decided to attempt Shishapangma, which is probably the only 8000-meter peak where skis offer an advantage. Since Nicole is a passionate skier, this was right up her alley. In order to save time and money, we joined a commercial expedition organized by Swiss expedition operator Kari Kobler. We would benefit from Kobler's infrastructure up to and at base camp but would be autonomous higher up on the mountain. On my previous expeditions I had always traveled to Tibet via the road from Nepal so I had never had the chance to visit Lhasa. During our time in the Tibetan capital, Nicole and I took the opportunity to take in the cultural sights, or what was left of them after the Chinese invasion and cultural revolution. We were impressed by the palaces and monasteries in Lhasa, Shigatse, and Shegar. I was absolutely fascinated because I had never really spent much time delving into Tibetan culture.

After a few days, though, I had seen enough palaces and could not wait to move again. The road network, which compared to Nepal was very well developed, and the Tibetans' entrepreneurial spirit surprised me and made me realize that the Chinese influence was not always negative. On the sixth day of our road trip, we reached Chinese base camp, which at 5000 meters is accessible by car. From there we walked upstream to the real base camp; at 5600 meters it is pretty high but still on the moraine and not on the snow.

Nicole and I set out for base camp a day before the rest of the team. We wanted to get settled in our temporary home. We had not anticipated that the yaks would take a lot longer than us and that we would get there way ahead of our gear. However, with Norbu at base camp, it was not half as bad as it might have been since he offered us tea and shelter until our stuff arrived. Norbu Sherpa had started his career as kitchen boy and then advanced to climbing Sherpa and sirdar. He had just set up his own company and was now organizing the "Double 8 expedition"—an expedition in which the members would climb both Shishapangma and Cho Oyu in one season. We spent all afternoon drinking tea and discussing plans with the expedition members after they arrived. Benedikt Böhm and Sebastian Haag from Munich, famous for their speed climbs using skis, their compatriot Martin Meier, and the Italian Andrea Zambaldi were planning to climb both Shishapangma and Cho Oyu within one week and get from base camp to base camp by bike. I was impressed by their very ambitious goal.

Our gear arrived just in time for Nicole and me to pitch our tent and go to sleep. We spent the following day sorting our things before the last of the crew arrived in the evening. Expedition life had begun. During our first acclimatization rotation, Nicole and I climbed up to Camp 1 with me carrying quite a heavy load. I wanted to make our Camp 1 as comfortable as possible in order to feel good during our acclimatization and not lose motivation and energy. The conditions turned out to be pretty good, with not too much snow, at least down there.

After we had spent our first night at Camp 1, I carried a load to Camp 2 the following day while Nicole was resting and acclimatizing. We had already agreed before the expedition that I would do the lion's share of the work, such as carrying loads and pitching tents. If Nicole had been required to carry a sixty-pound backpack she would not have stood a chance. This was not a problem since this expedition was not about my ambition (I had indulged that when I soloed the South Face in 2011) but about Nicole and me reaching the summit together.

At 6900 meters I pitched our Camp 2 and then put on my skis and set off. Skiing down was fun and efficient, even though it was not completely effortless at this altitude. I am not an exceptionally gifted skier, but I am sure it was not only poor technique that made it challenging. After about fifteen minutes I was back at Camp 1, where Nicole was waiting for me with a cup of tea.

The following day we climbed to Camp 2 together. My heavy bag was weighing on my shoulders again, and when Beni and Basti came toward us I glanced enviously at their tiny backpacks. They had also climbed to Camp 2 from Camp 1 that morning. They used a different acclimatization technique: not sleeping higher than Camp 1 but going on day trips to higher altitudes. I am sure that their strategy worked well, but it required top fitness. Climbing with Nicole, it was better to ascend more slowly and sleep at Camp 2. As usual, the first night this high, at 6900 meters, was uncomfortable. Our bodies had not yet acclimatized to the thin air. Once you fall asleep up here, your heart rate drops and you do not get sufficient oxygen. Usually, though, the body gets used to this phenomenon after the first night. The following morning we spoiled ourselves with a good cup of French press coffee before we decided to go back to base camp and not stay at Camp 2 as initially planned. The weather was deteriorating, and our bodies had already benefited from being up high for this short period of time.

During our next acclimatization rotation, we stayed one night at Camp 1 and one night at Camp 2. Since we felt well acclimatized and strong, we decided to carry on to Camp 3 at 7300 meters and then, if we continued to feel well, attempt the summit the next day. Since the Double 8 team intended to go for the summit a day ahead of us, we knew we could benefit from their tracks. While Nicole and I were plodding up the endlessly long valley leading up to Camp 3, I was imagining Beni, Basti, Martin, and Andrea reaching the summit soon. However, just as we were reaching the end of the valley, Basti and Beni skied toward us near Camp 3. "Too much snow," they said disappointedly. The avalanche danger was too high, and breaking trail had been exhausting.

After we exchanged a few words, they continued skiing down. Nicole and I took stock of the situation and came to the conclusion that if the four speed climbers could not make it, we would have little or no chance of reaching the summit. As I had all the gear for Camp 3 in my backpack, I wanted to continue on and leave it up there, but I did not want to leave Nicole to ski down to base camp on her own. At that moment Martin and Andrea came down on their skis and agreed Nicole could go with them. I carried on to Camp 3, dumped our gear, and then turned back and followed them.

In the evening the whole team was reunited at base camp. Nicole and I were now well acclimatized, with a good base for the next weather window. We had been there for twelve days and had twenty more days at our disposal. There was plenty of time to reach the summit, which was reassuring. Before we could achieve anything, though, the conditions had to improve high up on the mountain. Getting to Camp 3 in the loose, deep snow was pretty exhausting for me in these conditions, which meant that Nicole would have no chance of reaching the summit. We had to wait for the snow to settle or get blown off. With all the waiting, we had a lot of time for each other. Apart from eating, drinking, sleeping, reading, and watching an occasional DVD, there was not much to do.

Unfortunately the conditions on the mountain did not improve for days. There was still too much snow, and, despite the fair weather, the constant cold wind prevented the snow from settling. There was no point in attempting the summit with Nicole since it would have been far too strenuous for her. The Double 8 team was beginning to run out of time since they had the second project ahead of them so they decided to give it another go. If it did not work out this time, they would just continue to Cho Oyu. Beni asked me whether I'd like to join them since this would give me my desperately needed exercise and them an extra pair of legs for breaking trail. I liked the idea of shortening the waiting period, but I wanted to discuss it with Nicole since this was our trip. I was pretty sure she would not like the idea, so I was surprised when she encouraged me to join them. She said that there was not much to do at base camp anyway, and if I went with them then I would know in advance what it was like up there. As soon as the snow conditions improved, the two of us would give it another go at Nicole's pace.

Given the amount of snow, the Double 8 team changed their strategy slightly. Their original plan was for the whole team to go directly from base camp to the summit. Basti had now decided to go from Camp 1, while Andrea and Martin would leave from Camp 2. Only Beni stuck to the original plan of going directly from base camp. I decided to climb with Beni since I preferred to go directly from base camp myself. I would turn around at 7000 meters if I had to. Even though I had not been at my physical best that year, I liked the idea of ascending 2400 vertical meters and climbing one horizontal kilometer in a single day. It would be good training, in any case. I was very excited since I had never attempted an 8000-meter peak on skis. I hoped that

I would be able to keep up. Beni and his friends were top athletes and extremely skillful at ski mountaineering.

▲ ▲ ▲

Beni and I headed out of base camp in the late afternoon of September 23, intending to meet the others, who were already higher up, the following morning. We would then join forces and go for the summit together. As we had a long mission ahead of us, we took it easy and moved at a speed that allowed us to hold a conversation. We wanted to cross the glacier in daylight since finding the route through the maze of ice towers and crevasses would have been difficult in the dark.

I had suggested to Beni that we should wear running shoes all the way to the ski deposit at 5800 meters. Crossing the glacier was not difficult and in my view absolutely doable without crampons. Even though we would be using superlight ski boots, I preferred running shoes to ski boots and crampons since the soft sole of the running shoes stuck pretty well to the ice. Without too much effort we crossed the glacier significantly faster than we had when wearing ski boots.

We reached the ski deposit at dusk. Here the wind had swept the snow off the glacier. Once we started moving up the glacier on skis, we needed to adopt a completely new rhythm. Scurrying through the night, we could already see the light at Camp 1 at 6300 meters from afar. Once we got there we crawled into Basti's tent and had some of the tea he had prepared for us. It felt good to take a break, have a hot drink, and eat a chocolate bar. As planned, the three of us left Camp 1 at 8:00 p.m., while Martin and Andrea left Camp 2 for the summit at exactly the same time.

We were making good progress. It was only 600 meters of ascent to Camp 2, where I took a short break to put on my boot heaters, which I had left there. I had been a little ahead of Basti and Beni, but they passed my tent while I was having a quick drink and a bite to eat. I then stepped back into the night and followed them. From here the route led through a long flat valley, and I could see the faint light of Andrea's and Martin's headlamps at the end of it. Catching up with Basti and Beni took a lot of effort, but the three of us were reunited again just before the terrain got steeper approaching Camp 3. Martin and Andrea had broken a good trail and had stayed on the ridge and not in the couloir, which still had a lot of snow. Because it was safer, we took off our skis and continued on foot. Just below Camp 3, at about 1:00 a.m., we caught up with Andrea and Martin.

We reached Camp 3 at 7300 meters at about 2:00 a.m. We were well on track and had only another 700 meters of climbing to reach the summit. We all felt very optimistic and motivated and were happy that we had already come this far. We ought to be able to make it, we thought, given that we were taking turns breaking trail. The descent would be pretty quick since we would be able to ski down the lower part. We stopped for a while and discussed the situation. We all agreed that we had to be extremely careful not to trigger any avalanches. We knew that it was important to stay on the ridge and not step onto the slope. Because of the avalanche danger we would not be able to ski down from the summit as planned but would have to walk back down on the ridge. At camp we deposited our skis and I put on the down suit that I had left there. I probably would not get cold as long as I was breaking trail, but I knew that once I was at the back and walking slowly, at the pace of the person breaking trail, I would probably get cold and would appreciate the warmer gear. I also realized that I was starting to get tired, which was not surprising since Beni and I had essentially been on the go for ten hours.

Even though we were aware of the looming dangers, we all agreed to continue. In some places we could hardly make any progress digging through the hip-deep snow, while in other parts it was quite easy and we moved fairly quickly. The man in front would dig until he was panting and gasping for breath, and then another would take a turn. Fortunately there were five of us, and we could motivate each other to continue.

Just before 7:00 a.m. we had reached a point about 100 meters below the central summit, which was our goal. I looked up, thinking that it looked like we could do it. We had just taken turns breaking trail when I stopped for a second, took an energy bar from my pocket, and had a sip to drink. Beni and I had departed from base camp fourteen hours and forty minutes earlier.

Andrea was below me, and Beni, Basti, and Martin were about 10 meters above me, with Beni a little bit closer to the ridge than Martin and Basti. All of a sudden I heard a soft *whoomph*, and the ground beneath and next to me started to move. A slab avalanche! The snow started to move below me, but I was able to keep my balance. Everything happened very quickly. I saw two people slide down past me, saw Beni above me, and looked down, calling for Andrea. But there was no reply. Only Beni and I were there, where seconds earlier there had been five of us. And now Basti, Martin, and Andrea were all gone!

Beni came down to join me. We tried to come to terms with what had just happened. About 100 meters of the width of the slope had moved, and the tear-off line was about half a meter high. A gigantic volume of snow had thundered down over the seracs for 500 or 600 meters. Now what should we do? What were the chances of surviving in such a mass of heavy snow?

I took the radio from Beni and called down to base camp. Beni was trembling. Basti, who was his best friend and had been his climbing and skiing partner for many years, was now probably dead. I was unable to reach base camp. We would have to try again a little bit farther down. From where we were we could just see the place where the avalanche had broken off, but we were unable to make out whether there was anybody on the surface.

We retraced our steps down the ridge. As soon as I was able to get a radio connection, I informed Norbu about the avalanche and told him that we did not know what had happened to the other three. We would search for them farther down, but he should get ready for a rescue operation and mobilize help. I also asked him to tell Nicole as well as Suzanne Hüsser, who was guiding Kari Kobler's team.

Despite its being far below us, we were able to get a fair view of the gigantic avalanche debris just above Camp 3. We stopped and scanned the slope below us with our eyes. Suddenly we could make out two colored dots, one of which was moving. Slowly, yes, but it was moving: there was someone on top of the debris and not buried by it. Someone was alive! We shouted but heard no reply, and continued to descend. Crossing directly from where we were was simply impossible. The slope was steep and loaded with snow, with the same exposure as higher up. If we stepped onto the slope here we would trigger another avalanche. We had to be patient. Maybe we would have a better chance lower down.

After I informed base camp about the situation, we continued to descend. Beni and I decided to fetch the skis from Camp 3 and try to get to the avalanche debris lower down. Beni hurried ahead while I packed up a few things from the camp and followed him. Beni then started traversing just below the gigantic flank. The snow did not feel right, nor did our gut feeling. We retreated and discussed the situation again. Maybe it would be better higher up after all? We ascended a bit and tried to traverse again. We kept a good distance between us for safety reasons, but we sank into bottomless snow and had no other choice than to turn back again.

What to do? Both Beni and I were scared. It was far too dangerous to step onto the slope lower down. We climbed up to the rib, from which we could see the debris quite well. The slope leading up to it looked loaded with drift, the same as before. Should we try anyway despite the avalanche danger? We were torn between going and staying put. There were only two possibilities: the slope either moved or it held. We would survive or die. It was a desperate situation.

The little dot that had moved before had been motionless for about half an hour. I looked up. It was about 600 meters up to the ridge where the avalanche had broken off. It had been a long fall.

I radioed down to Suzanne at base camp. I tried to describe the situation as precisely as possible for her to give me some advice as a mountain guide. Without hesitating she said: "Don't go!" I was desperate, and so was Beni. Suddenly he said: "I am going over. I'm going." "Beni, calm down," I replied. "There is no point in us stepping onto the slope and triggering another avalanche. There will only be two more dead bodies."

A lot of time had passed, and we probably could no longer do anything for anyone caught under the snow. Suffocation was likely by now, even if the fall itself had not been fatal. But what about the colored dot that had been moving before? Who was it? I now assumed that the person lying there was probably dead by now. But I did not know. I felt like crying. This was the worst situation I had ever been in.

I radioed down to Suzanne again. She urged me to be sensible and said we should not do anything stupid. We were still torn. We waited, trying to find a solution. But there was none.

Just before noon we decided to go down to Camp 3. Five hours had passed since the avalanche had come down. There was nothing we could do now. If one of them had really survived and was able to move on his own, he would either be lucky and not trigger an avalanche—or die. A brutal thought. I found it hard to make this decision. Once again Beni and I tried to run through what had happened. We could not turn back time, and the risk of triggering another avalanche was too great for us to traverse on the slope. We had discussed the avalanche danger during the ascent, which was the reason why we had decided to stay on the ridge. With the sun getting more intense and the snow softening, the risk was even higher now. There were too many arguments against a rescue attempt. But this would mean abandoning our friends to their fate.

Beni tried one last time to step onto the slope but immediately turned back. He was up to his hips in the soft snow. It was impossible! We descended to Camp 3. I radioed down to base camp to discuss the situation with Norbu. He told me that there were enough people to help at Camp 2 and Camp 1 and that we should come down. Just to be on the safe side, I left my down suit and stove in our tent. I thought that if one of the others actually survived the avalanche, he would have some food and something warm to get by for a while.

Beni and I started to head down toward base camp, neither of us able to speak. Beni was distraught. He had just lost his best friend and knew that Basti's parents would be devastated. Only a few years before their older son had died in the mountains. For the last time, I turned around and had another look at the slope. I had never had to make such a difficult decision in my life.

Between Camp 1 and Camp 2 a few Sherpas came toward us and gave us some tea. At Camp 1 we met the team of the Spanish veteran climber Carlos Soria. Among the others was a medical doctor; it was good to know that in case one of them had survived and managed to get out, there was a doctor on the mountain. Our guys had a radio with them and could call for help. Something inside me did not want to give up the hope that someone had survived the avalanche.

On the further descent Beni and I went completely to pieces. We were extremely tired and struggling to make progress. We kept stopping to discuss the situation. Why did people have to die again? Damned mountaineering! Why were we still here and the others gone? It was simply luck. We should have turned back earlier. Of course we should have, but it is always easier to say in hindsight. We had misjudged the situation.

After we had traversed the pinnacles some Sherpas came toward us and gave us some drink and food. Finally I saw Nicole approaching. Seeing her was a huge relief.

Just before we reached base camp, the radio came to life again and there was a frenzy of talking. Thomas, a member of the Swiss expedition with whom we were sharing base camp, had gone up a little higher in the afternoon and had seen something move in the avalanche debris. One of them was still alive and was moving toward Camp 3! Norbu and two other Sherpas immediately set out to help. It was evening by now, and Beni and I had been on our feet for twenty-four hours. We were too tired to go back up—and it would have taken us ages. But at least there was hope!

The three Sherpas climbed to Camp 2 in the night and carried on the following morning. Just below Camp 3 Norbu continued on his own, as he deemed the steep section too risky to put three people into danger. Once he got there he found the survivor inside the tent. It was Martin. He had regained consciousness sometime in the afternoon and been able to drag himself to Camp 3. Traversing the avalanche-prone slope was the only way for him to survive. Fortunately he had not triggered another avalanche and managed to reach the tent after night had fallen. He had at least been able to cover himself with my down suit, but he had been too exhausted to get the stove going.

It was a miracle that he had survived the fall. He had partially torn a knee meniscus, sprained a few muscles in his legs, and stretched a few ligaments, but these were relatively mild injuries. He did not get frostbite, but he had suffered a concussion and had double vision. He responded to Norbu, but he was unable to walk on his own. Joining forces, Norbu and some members of the Spanish expedition managed to get him down to Camp 2 on his skis. There, the Spanish doctor gave him such a dose of amphetamine that he was able to descend to base camp on his own the next day. Martin was incredibly tough, and the first thing he wanted when he got to base camp was a cigarette. Despite our grief for Basti and Andrea, Beni and I were happy that at least one of the three had survived.

▲▲▲

This was the end of our expedition, and on our trip home my thoughts tortured me. Something had happened again, and people had lost their lives. Why was it that I went mountaineering? Nicole too struggled with this. Why didn't we do something less dangerous? Why not go on a beach holiday? Should we give up mountaineering? But like me she was feeling conflicted. In climbing we had each experienced our most beautiful and intense moments, experiences a beach holiday could never give us. It is hard for me to imagine a life without mountaineering.

In my early climbing days I had faced the fact that friends died in the mountains. At the time, however, it had not really sunk in, and I was convinced that it would never affect me. However, the more and harder I climbed, the more often I was faced with precarious situations. Over the past few years it seemed that such instances happened with increased frequency. I had taken great risks on Annapurna. I had come back alive, but I did not know how close I had been to the limit. On Shishapangma I had simply been lucky. If I had not stopped to take a break just before the avalanche came down, I would have been closer to Martin and Basti and would have probably been swept away with them. The fact that I was a bit lower down and slightly to the right had saved my life. My gut feeling had warned me that something wasn't right, but still I had continued.

After our Shishapangma expedition I was fed up with mountaineering for a while. I doubted my ability to make the right decisions. I knew that I should have turned back up there, but there was no point now in wondering about culpability. Five of us had been up there, and we all knew what was going on—we had discussed the avalanche danger beforehand. Each of us was responsible for his own actions, and each of us had to bear the consequences. Any one of us could have turned back. But we had all carried on and gone too far. Now two were dead.

Only a few weeks earlier Nicole and I had been extremely lucky on the Artesonraju in Peru. After we climbed the

South Face we descended via the east ridge, which led us down a slope of 40 to 50 degrees, covered in hard snow. It had been windy all day, and I was nervous about the snow that had been blown onto the slope. I was very careful not to end up in a hidden drift. Just above the bergschrund I lowered Nicole over two 30-meter pitches and then climbed down myself. Everything went smoothly, and I felt relieved after we had crossed the bergschrund. From here the slope petered out, and we only had to cross the glacier to get to our camp.

I started traversing the slope at an angle. Nicole was on a tight rope and walking about 30 meters behind me. Suddenly there was a bang. A slab avalanche. A crack of about 10 meters had opened up right above me. It was not that much snow, but it was enough to throw me off balance, and Nicole could not hold me. I started sliding and dragged her down with me even though she had been above the crack and had not been touched by the avalanche. The snow pulled me toward a crevasse, and I could see the snow disappear into it. "This is it," I thought. "It's the end." I thought about Nicole and hoped that she would survive.

Headfirst, I plunged into the crevasse. It was not very deep, and when I hit the ground the snow pressed me toward the right. Suddenly I stopped, but more snow kept on falling, burying me. There was nothing I could do. It was dark, my body was twisted, and I was barely able to breathe. I had no idea how deeply I was buried, but I could not move and felt like I was encased in concrete. My mouth was full of snow, and when I inhaled it went down my windpipe. Luckily I managed to spit out the snow—there was a tiny space just in front of my mouth. I could see light coming through a hole. I gasped a little air, but that was it. I was convinced that I would die there under the snow. I had failed myself and Nicole!

At this moment a foot stomped through the opening. Nicole was directly above me. I wanted to say something but I could not utter a word. She had been able to stay above the avalanche, and when she saw my ice axe sticking out of the snow, she started digging there immediately. She first removed the snow from my face and then dug me out completely.

That had been a close call, and I had made a wrong decision. I had not realized that the slope had actually been a big dip covered in snow. I had been negligent, which had nearly cost both of us our lives. I was very angry at myself and beat myself up over it. Making bad decisions for myself was one thing, but putting other people in danger was another. When I was in the mountains with Nicole, who has a lot less experience than me, I was in charge and needed to act responsibly.

At times you make such mistakes, no matter how good an alpinist you are. The more time you spend in the mountains, the longer you move on dangerous ground, the likelier it is that you'll make a mistake. Of course, some mountaineers take more risks than others, but risk increases with frequency. I am convinced of this. And keeping this in mind I adapted my training and started to keep fit by running rather than climbing challenging alpine routes. But even running presents risk, especially if it is running up the Mönch from Grindelwald, which I still do every once in a while, especially when I'm bored of more horizontal running. Even though it is the normal route, it is still exposed. For that matter, I am not immune when I run down the easy hill just outside my house. Sometimes my foot gets caught up in something and I trip, but on such terrain a fall does not have fatal consequences. A fall at the wrong moment, in the wrong place, and it's all over. Everyone has to be aware of that and decide how much risk to take on.

Why had we gone that far and accepted the high avalanche danger on Shishapangma? I don't believe that the Himalaya are inherently more dangerous than the Alps, even though they bear the added risk of altitude illness. The jeopardy lies within ourselves. One reason we take more risks in the Himalaya is because climbing there requires organization long in advance and costs more money and time. That's why we sometimes set out even in dangerous conditions just to "have a quick look." I have done this many times in the past. It often works out even though neither the weather nor the conditions are ideal, but it pushes you closer to the critical border. For me as a Swiss climber there is no need to set out in bad conditions in the Alps. If I don't go now, I go soon, when the conditions are better. If not this year, then next year. For us Europeans getting there is less of an ordeal, and that's why making the decision to turn around there is easier.

I think that's where big expeditions sometimes go wrong. You should be brave enough to say no and not go when the conditions are not right. I had been very careful not to succumb to outside pressure, such as from sponsors, and risk making bad decisions, but I realize now that a lot of pressure came from within myself. In order to counteract this danger, I had to learn not to let the urge to "go and have a look" control my actions. Had I decided against going with Beni, Basti, Andrea, and Martin to have a look, I would not have put myself into this situation. Had we been in the Alps, I probably would have said: "No thanks. I'd rather go rock climbing."

▲ ▲ ▲

My year of climbing with Nicole was coming to an end. Since I was doing a lot of presentations in November and December and traveling to the United States for a ten-day tour, we extended our holiday and spent January and the first half of February 2015 in Chamonix. Nicole had given me freeride skis for Christmas with the intention of getting me more excited about her passion for gliding down deep powder snow. In addition to skiing, we climbed a few cool ice routes, such as the North Couloir Direct on the Dru and the *Late to Say I'm Sorry* route on the Aiguille Verte. I also started training with ultralight touring skis. I liked the idea of getting down quickly after having climbed high. As always, I felt motivated by Chamonix. It's a mecca for motivated mountaineers, and I felt inspired by their energy.

I still felt I needed to find direction again. Driven by the sense that I had reached my peak, I needed a new perspective. What was there left to do? Slowly the fire inside me started to grow again. In my fantasy I was hedging and started to train more seriously again, especially for ultra runs. During one of my sponsor events in Chamonix, I met Catalan trail runner Kilian Jornet and was fascinated by his performance and attitude. Running 50 kilometers per day was not a big deal for him. And what he described as an easy run was beyond what most runners do. His physical condition was phenomenal, and I was far from it. His performance, however, motivated me to train harder. When he climbed the Lion Ridge on the Matterhorn, he covered 1277 meters per hour! I would have to train hard to come anywhere near that. During my speed climb on the Eiger North Face, I covered 600 meters per hour. On the Grandes Jorasses, a technically difficult climb that was unknown to me, I managed 500 meters per hour.

We were back home for Nicole's birthday on February 19. As a special birthday treat, I agreed to go ski mountaineering with her. I really don't like skiing all that much and only do it to make Nicole happy. I cannot get excited about it. With the standard equipment, it does not really have a training effect, and the only benefit I see is getting to the start of the climb. With the ultralight equipment, however, I was at least able to run up quickly, which was fun. On Nicole's birthday tour my mediocre skiing skills were unfortunately not up to coping with the difficult crusted snow conditions. At one point I dug in one of the edges wrong, fell, and fractured a bone just above my right ankle. This brought me back to reality. My outstanding physical fitness was no longer important, and for the time being I had to stop dreaming about future projects. I had to stop dreaming of running the 111-kilometer ultramarathon in Portugal and the 50-mile race at Lake Sonoma, not to mention all my climbing plans for the Alps for March.

At first I was devastated, but then I pulled myself together. My coach, Simon Trachsel, adapted my training program. Instead of training outside I went to the gym and used a spinning bike instead of running. I wanted to fully use my potential for endurance. I was aware that at the age of thirty-eight I did not have the same body as a twenty-year-old. What I did have, though, were years of experience, and I knew what I wanted. My focus was clear. I wanted to continue climbing 8000-meter peaks, but I wanted to scale them via technically demanding routes. I was dreaming about routes such as the West Face of Makalu, where high altitude was a big part of the challenge. Here I could see some potential to improve my performance. On the lower part of the South Face of Annapurna, I had covered a ridiculous 200 meters per hour, and this had been reduced to 150 meters per hour on the upper part. During my preparation climb on the Peuterey Intégral, I had done 500 meters per hour. Trying to figure out how to get faster, I had a closer look at Kilian's performance. On the Innominata Ridge of

Mont Blanc, he had covered barely more than 375 meters per hour on the technical sections. This gave me hope. He was certainly a better endurance athlete, but I was definitely the better technical climber. I worked out that his endurance combined with my technical skills, which quickly got me over difficult sections using my hands and feet, would probably result in covering up to 800 meters per hour.

I wanted to pursue this goal, but I had to withdraw from public life in order to achieve it in my own time and without any outside pressure. A first step in that direction was to allow myself to realize a long-cherished project in the summer of 2015: to climb all eighty-two 4000-meter peaks in the Alps. This was nothing new and had been done many times before. It was also nothing crazy, since most summits could be reached via a normal route. But I wanted to do it. I would cover a lot of vertical and horizontal kilometers. Not too long ago I would have worried about people accusing me of getting old and only pursuing such goals to attract media attention. Now I couldn't care less what others were thinking.

I was planning to return to the Himalaya in the autumn of 2015 to keep my high-altitude fitness. In 2003 Russian climber Valery Babanov had opened a new route on the South Face of Nuptse, but he had used fixed lines. All attempts to repeat his feat in alpine style had failed so far. I was convinced that with today's advanced technical skills and gear this route could be done without fixed ropes from base camp straight to the summit. It was an appealing challenge.

However, before I could realize all these ideas, I would have to bear down and continue to go to the gym for a few more weeks. Such was life. The foot would heal, and I would definitely be more motivated afterward. Sometimes you need setbacks to make you aware of what you have achieved and what you still want to achieve.

ALL 4000-METER PEAKS IN THE ALPS REDISCOVERING THE JOY OF CLIMBING

The most appealing aspect of climbing all eighty-two 4000-meter peaks in the Alps was that this project was right at my doorstep. During my time as a professional alpinist I had visited many mountain ranges in the world. By now I had been to the Himalaya so many times that I knew Kathmandu almost as well as my hometown, Interlaken. But I was super excited about climbing on my own stomping grounds and discovering a few places in the Alps I had never seen.

French climber Patrick Berhault was my inspiration for this. With his partner Philippe Magnin he set out in March 2004 to climb all 4000-meter peaks in the Alps in three months. Tragically, Patrick fell to his death on his way to his sixty-seventh summit, when a cornice collapsed on the traverse from the Täschhorn to the Dom. Three years later, in 2007, Slovenian climber Miha Valič became the first person to finish the grand traverse, reaching the eighty-two summits in 102 days. In 2008 Italians Franco Nicolini and Diego Giovannini reached the eighty-two summits in just sixty days.

When climbing peak after peak successively within a few weeks, one is subject to the whims of the weather. I knew that I would have to deal with bad weather during this mission and weather would be the deciding factor in how quickly I would be able to do it. As I wanted to avoid climbing in bad conditions, which would have exposed me to greater risks, I did not want this traverse to turn into a race. I had made my name with speed records and had benefited from the public's reaction to this, but after recent events I wanted to keep speed out of my projects. Comparing mountaineering achievements is difficult anyway, since the climber's performance depends on the conditions on the mountain.

I had found another challenge, though. I wanted to do the whole distance, including traveling between mountains, using only the power of my own body. Instead of a car, I would use a bike to reach the base of each peak, and I would not take cable cars to shorten the ascents. The only thing I would allow myself would be to paraglide down from a summit, wherever and whenever possible. I did not count that as mechanical support. I imagined the eighty-two summits project to be a journey through the Alps, more about the experience than about the performance. I will admit, though, that the physical challenge had a huge appeal to me. Would my body be able to endure such a long, stressful endeavor? The slightest injury or inflammation would mean the end. Something that would be tolerable on a one- or two-day outing could lead to fatality on a traverse of sixty to eighty days. One could take on such a challenge only if one's body were strong enough to recover quickly.

The mental challenge also excited me. Would I be able to stay motivated over such a long time and for such a long distance? What would happen if things were not going smoothly? Would I throw in the towel? Failure was definitely a possibility, but facing it made the whole project even more appealing.

I asked young German mountain guide Michael Wohlleben if he would be interested in joining me. In the winter of 2014 I had climbed the north faces of the Drei Zinnen in the Dolomites in Italy with him, and we had been a good team. Formerly a member of the youth section of the German Alpine Club, Michi (as he calls himself) was in the process of establishing himself as a professional mountaineer. He liked the idea of the 4000-meter traverse and said yes immediately. Since Michi was a paraglider, we made a perfect team.

Such a big project required a lot of planning and organizing. First we had to decide the order in which we would climb the mountains. As we would be traveling by bicycle, our options were limited. We could not just quickly go from the Bernese Oberland to the Valais if weather conditions made that clearly preferable. We had to accept that there would probably be waiting periods. We agreed to start with Piz Bernina, the easternmost mountain in the Alps. But what would be the best way to get to the Bernese Oberland after that? Neither Michi nor I were big cyclists. We tried to calculate distances as well as elevation gains: How many kilometers a day was realistic?

The next step was finding support. We needed a support vehicle and a person to transport our gear. Daniel Mader, an old friend of mine, had been enthusiastic about the project from the very beginning, and it didn't take long to convince him to be our support and logistics person. This made me very happy since Dani is not only extremely reliable, he is also always motivated and in good spirits. Renting a camper van for the duration of the project would have been too pricy, but my brother Bruno and his wife agreed to swap their big VW van for my car. Michi also arranged for a trailer that the van could tow.

Bikes were the only thing left to sort out. I called Thomas Binggeli of the Swiss bike manufacturer BMC; he got so excited about our plan that he offered us two high-tech bikes about five minutes into our conversation. Thomas did not need a comprehensive presentation. He liked the idea and was in. I have to admit that I am a gear freak, and I love developing well-thought-through products with my sponsors. But I had not expected to be using such high-performance bikes. The riding experience would be awesome.

Now that things were all set, we got in touch with the media about our project. Michi and I had not focused on a time frame, knowing that the duration of the project was impossible to calculate due to weather and not wanting to pressure ourselves. But when journalists asked the inevitable question, "How long will it take?" we said eighty-two summits in eighty-two days. Bagging a peak per day seemed realistic.

▲ ▲ ▲

The conditions in the Alps were still too wintery. Before I started the eighty-two summits project, Nicole and I embarked on the last long trip of our sabbatical. She had found a new job and was due to start her position at the Swiss Post in July. Considering how many interesting jobs Nicole had had since I first met her, it seemed almost boring that I was still going climbing. But I did not want it any other way. I was leading exactly the life I had always dreamed about.

We flew to Utah, where we wanted to improve our skills in crack climbing on sandstone. I've always liked going to the States with its open and easygoing people. The land-scape is extremely diverse and completely different from ours. In Europe we do not have such orange or yellow rock formations covered with climbable parallel cracks that come in all shapes and sizes. In the States climbing is still more traditional. Most routes are not bolted, and the climbers have to put in their own protection, using cams or nuts. I really like this kind of climbing since it requires experience and a good eye for choosing the right-sized piece of gear from your rack. What's more, crack climbing demands a technique that is completely different from that of the wall climbing ubiquitous in Europe.

Life at Indian Creek, the climbing mecca in southeastern Utah, turned out to be pretty relaxing. We did not have a mobile phone signal or internet. It was an ideal place to find some peace and quiet and concentrate on the moment. We set up our camp in the middle of the desert. With the eighty-two summits project in mind, I went for a run or a bike ride every morning after breakfast. The mental and geographical distance from my normal life also made for better training. In the afternoons Nicole and I would go rock climbing, and in the evening we'd cook a meal together and go to sleep. I loved the simplicity of this life. The change was also good for my motivation. Had I only trained in Switzerland, I probably would have lost my enthusiasm at some point, even though my home was ideal for training. There are mountains, excellent running and biking routes, climbing crags, and a gym all in the vicinity of our house.

Utah was the perfect place to finish our sabbatical year. At the end of May 2015, we returned to Switzerland and were both full of energy. Nicole was very motivated about her new job, and I couldn't wait to tackle the eighty-two summits. The conditions in the Alps were pretty good, and Michi and I did not wait long to start. Both van and trailer were jam-packed with our gear, and our journey through the Swiss, French, and Italian Alps could begin.

▲ ▲ ▲

On June 11, 2015, Michi and I reached our first 4000-meter peak, climbing Piz Bernina via the Bianco Ridge. In order to make a quick descent, we decided to paraglide down near the Rifugio Marco e Rosa. Unfortunately the wind came from the wrong direction, and without Michi's urging I wouldn't even have tried. We unpacked our super-light paragliders and attempted to take off, but it was about half an hour before the wind cooperated. In the end the effort definitely paid off. The flight was magnificent. We drifted effortlessly down the valley, with the Morteratsch Glacier beneath us—it was so much easier than walking! Michi landed at the nose of the glacier, while I managed to get farther, almost reaching Hotel Morteratsch. After we had had coffee and cake there, we started pedaling across the Julier Pass to Bivio, where our van and trailer were waiting for us on the roadside. This was our first camp, and we were off to a great start! I was very happy that we had finally tackled the project. We had scaled our first peak and had only eighty-one to go.

My brother René joined the project in Bivio and biked with us to the Bernese Oberland. This made me very happy. We hadn't done anything together like this for a long time. Eric Wilde, a passionate triathlete, joined the team the following morning. Eric was two meters tall and had broad shoulders, which made him the perfect man for drafting. We started out biking downhill, and I was once again amazed how fast our bikes were going. After the beautiful ride through the Rhine Valley, we stopped just before the Oberalp Pass to have lunch. We didn't look at the prices and were extremely relieved when Dani showed up just in time to pay the bill. On the pass we got caught in the rain. We were very happy when we reached Andermatt.

The following day it was still pouring down rain. We delayed the start, looked at the weather forecast and radar, and tried to identify a dry period. Unsuccessful, we eventually cycled back to the Bernese Oberland via the Furka and Grimsel passes. René and I raced each other down; his speedometer showed 91 kilometers per hour. The bikes' carbon frames were so sturdy that I hadn't noticed how fast we were going; there was no shaking. We did need to be careful, since the thin tires limited the braking performance of the bikes, but the roads were empty due to the rain, which allowed for some speeding. When we arrived in Innertkirchen, neither Eric nor Michi were in sight.

From Innertkirchen we decided to go to my house in Ringgenberg. The weather forecast was so bad that we had to wait, but there was no better place to wait than home. We cooked some dinner, as our project rules did not allow us to take a car or train to quickly get to a restaurant in Innertkirchen. We would have had to get on the bikes again. Given the weather and the fact that we still had many kilometers of riding ahead of us, we were more than happy to stay in.

As soon as the weather forecast looked better, my photographer friend Dan Patitucci came and biked with us to Grindelwald, where we started our walk up toward the Schreckhorn Hut in the pouring rain. After having enjoyed coffee and cake at the Bäregg Hut, Michi and I continued to the Schreckhorn Hut, while Dan went down. Since the hut was still unstaffed that early in the year, we cooked some food in the winter room and made a fire to warm up and to dry our soaked clothes.

Far too early, at 2:00 a.m., we were rudely awakened by the alarm clock. The Schreckhorn was one of the more challenging 4000-meter peaks. The previous year, Nicole and I had done the Schreckhorn–Lauteraarhorn traverse in perfect conditions. This time it looked completely different. The rocks were covered in a thin layer of ice. We even took the thin rope out of our pack for protection. We reached the summit at dawn, and the conditions were better on the ridge. The rock was dry, making for pretty smooth climbing, but the route all the way to the top of the Lauteraarhorn dragged. We were not making such good progress.

The descent route via the Schraubengang was covered in soft snow. I had never been on that route before and only knew that it had to veer off to the right at some point. However, I didn't see a single spot where we could have conveniently climbed down from the ridge, and suddenly we could not go any farther. We climbed back up for about ten minutes until we reached a rappelling sling, which I had thought was in the wrong place before. It turned out to be the right place from which to rappel. Once down, we had to negotiate a delicate flank covered in soft snow and some loose rock. I climbed down backward while Michi decided to rappel this section. Another ridge led us to the Gaagg Peak. From there we continued down to the hut, where we had deposited our paragliders.

The wind conditions seemed good enough to paraglide. We had packed our lightweight paragliders since we had initially planned to carry them to the top of the Gaagg, but after seeing the thick fog engulfing the summit on our way up, we had left them at the hut. I quickly sorted out my chute and launched myself easily. Michi needed more time to lay out his paraglider. He missed the airstream and had to wait a long time for the winds to be favorable again.

My flight started off quite calmly. I could have quickly gained some more height, but I was starving and wanted to get down as quickly as possible. I flew straight to the Bäregg Hut. I had already come down quite far, but I was sure I could make it down all the way to the end of the gorge. In the worst case, I would turn around and land below the Bäregg Hut. But as I came around the corner at the Bäregg Hut, my paraglider suddenly came to a halt when a strong wind came up the valley through the gorge. I was annoyed with myself. I shouldn't have been so impatient and should have gained some more height before going down. Should I fly back and land at the Bäregg Hut? I decided to keep on going and fly as far down the valley as I could. Unfortunately I did not get as far as the gorge and was forced to land on an old hiking path. It took some skill to negotiate my way through the trees, and while I was able to land, the chute got caught in a tree, ripping a hole in it. It didn't bother me too much since it could be repaired. The most important thing was that I was down and only had to walk for another ten minutes.

I still hadn't seen Michi up in the air. Maybe he had missed the right moment to take off and had been forced to walk down. When I reached the parking lot Dani was waiting, and I found that there was mobile phone coverage. I called Michi, who told me that he'd had to perform an emergency landing just below the Bäregg. He had hit the ground hard and had injured his rear end. Dani hiked up to Michi while I jogged to Grindelwald, where we were going to stay the night in a chalet. I unpacked my gear, hung it up to dry, and took a long shower. Michi arrived three hours later with a huge bruise on his backside.

The following morning we started at four. We were planning to climb the Mönch via the Nollen Route and then continue to the Jungfrau. We were carrying only light packs, two ice axes each, and our crampons. We didn't need a rope for the Nollen Route. I was excited since I finally had the chance to use new boots that had been designed for this project. The style was a hybrid between a running shoe and a mountaineering boot. The material was flexible enough for the foot to roll, while the midsole was hard enough to take crampons. As the way to Guggi Hut was good ground for running, mountaineering boots became necessary only from the Mönch Plateau. I had done the entire route in running shoes before, but the conditions had been perfect at the time, and that does not happen very often. On other occasions I used to take two kinds of shoes for this climb: running shoes to the plateau and light mountaineering boots for higher up. Now I had the perfect boot for both kinds of terrain.

On the flat, I started to jog. Michi was complaining about his pain. I tried to cheer him up, telling him that the pain would subside once the muscle had warmed up. I knew what I was talking about. I had a big bruise on my thigh from Ringgenberg, where I'd fallen off my bike after having to brake hard at high speed to avoid having a cameraman hit me with his car.

I slowed down a bit on the stretch up to the Kleine Scheidegg to give Michi a chance to catch up. I tried to encourage him to keep up by setting a reasonable pace. At the Eigergletscher station and on the way to the Guggi Hut, he fell behind again. At the plateau I waited for him for a while but quickly started to shiver since I had not brought enough warm clothes. I stopped again after the Nollen, where I took some photographs and video footage. Right after this, mist started to appear, and a cold wind picked up. Dani and Bruno Petroni, another friend, were already waiting for us on the top of the Mönch.

Together we descended via the normal route and continued to the Jungfraujoch (the col between the Jungfrau and Mönch), where we had a bite to eat. We didn't stop for long, though. Michi and I still wanted to continue to the Jungfrau. While we were crossing the glacier toward the Jungfrau, it started to snow. Michi wanted to turn back, but I was far too motivated to agree to that. Neither the snowfall nor the fog were very serious, and we were following the normal route. In a worst-case scenario we could use the GPS tracker on my watch to find our way back to the Jungfraujoch. Beyond the Rottalsattel we were hit by a gusty wind. I didn't mind at all—I like feeling the wind and the elements on my body—but Michi insisted on calling it a day since he thought it was too dangerous and foolhardy to carry on in such conditions. I understood that it was just too much for him. We were about 100 meters below the summit when we turned back and walked via the Jungfraujoch to the Mönchsjoch Hut. At least we had covered a lot of distance and climbed many meters, which made me feel rather satisfied.

As forecast, it snowed heavily the next day. We were stuck in the Mönchsjoch Hut. There was nothing we could do. I closely studied the weather radar, hoping to detect more moderate conditions. The forecast for June 20 looked somewhat more promising. There was supposed to be a dry spell between 1:00 a.m. and 6:00 a.m. I suggested to Michi that we make the most of this dry period and climb the Jungfrau during the night and rest during the day. When we left the hut, the sky was cloudy, and once we reached the Jungfraujoch we were engulfed in thick fog. Michi wanted to retreat again, but this time I insisted on continuing. Mist often lingers at the Jungfraujoch but clears higher up. When we reached the glacier, we could already see some stars. In the darkness I used my watch to get my bearings. Fortunately we had recorded the GPS data during our first attempt, which allowed us to follow the tracker, leading us to about 100 meters below the top of the Mönch.

The fresh snow that had fallen over the previous day, combined with the wind, meant we had to be extra careful under the Rottalsattel. To avoid the slipstream, where a lot of snow had gathered, we did not traverse as far right as usual but climbed directly up the Rottalsattel and continued to the summit ridge. This was where we had turned back before, but this time we continued to the top. I loved being up here in the middle of the night. The lights of Grindelwald were below us, the wind was howling, and my eyelashes were frosty. During our descent clouds were gathering, and it started to snow. It was fortunate that we had used that short weather window!

We were back at the Mönchsjoch Hut for our second breakfast and had nothing to do except sit around for the rest of the day. The weather forecast did not look promising. Westerly winds were forecast to dump heaps of fresh snow in the Bernese Oberland, and the whole week was looking dismal. If we waited here we would have to face fresh snow on the slopes. Being on skis would help, but we would still be exposed to the high avalanche danger. The forecast looked better for the Valais, but if we went down to the Valais now we would have to come back to the Bernese Oberland later. This would mean a huge detour on bike and foot, but this was certainly better than hanging around the hut doing nothing.

The following day we skied down the Jungfraujoch via the Aletsch Glacier to Fiesch. The fog was so thick we could barely see: a complete whiteout. We tied into a rope and I led the way. If a crevasse had opened up in front of me, I probably would have seen it only at the very last instant since I was unable to make out any contours in the landscape. I blindly followed my GPS, which we had programmed in the hut. Without any reference points I felt a bit queasy at times, not knowing even whether the slope was going up or down. Michi was tense again, and I tried to calm him down. If anyone fell into a crevasse it would be me, and it probably wouldn't be a big deal. It usually takes only a few minutes to get out.

At Concordia Place we were below the clouds and had a clear view again. There was not an inch of new snow left on the glacier, and skiing across it was bumpy but a lot better than walking. At Märjelen Lake we got off the glacier and walked down to the valley via the Fiescheralp. It was still early and we could have easily gone to Saas-Grund the same day, but Michi's family had come to visit and was waiting for him in Fiesch. It was a shame, as we ended up spending the nicest day of the week biking to Saas-Grund with them instead of climbing.

I sensed that Michi was not fit and that something was bothering him. In the evening after the bike ride, he came to the trailer and told me that he had decided go home since he was hurting too much to continue. I was surprised to hear that his injury was so serious, although I had noticed that Michi had been slower than usual. I tried to convince him to continue and begged him to sleep on it before making a final decision.

I slept badly that night. I was disappointed. What would happen to the project if Michi left? I didn't want to give up. Ending a project like this was not my style, but how could I possibly manage on my own?

The next morning Michi told me rather bluntly that he would go home with his family. At first, I couldn't believe it, but I had no choice but to accept it. I guess it was not only the injury that led to his decision but also the realization that our attitudes differed when it came to accepting risks. Michi had less experience on mixed ground than he did on rock.

I wanted to carry on, no matter what. I simply could not give up after just five summits, neither as a professional climber nor because of my personal ambitions. I was looking for a way to continue without Michi, maybe with several different partners.

Michi said goodbye at noon, and Dani and I ascended to the Weissmies Hut in the late afternoon. Walking felt good, and I could breathe deeply again. We just continued on as if nothing had happened. Deep down I was hoping that Michi would come back once his bruise had healed. We would see. I tried to adapt to the new situation and not worry too much.

▲ ▲ ▲

The next morning Dani and I climbed the Lagginhorn together; on the summit, we bid each other farewell. While Dani returned to the hut, I continued climbing the ridge to the Weissmies. I truly enjoyed the beautiful climbing and getting back into my rhythm. Once on the summit I felt good and confident again. I was sure that there was a solution, even if Michi had dropped out. I knew enough good alpinists to hook up with. It was only a matter of them having time for me and me having to make some phone calls and do some organizing in the next few weeks. The descent was quick. From the hut I continued to the middle cable car station, where Dani was waiting for me. He'd rounded up two kick scooters, and we quickly zoomed down the valley on them.

My climbing friend Röbi Bösch had arrived in the meantime, and the three of us set out toward the Mischabel Hut. Röbi and Dani took the cable car. I ran and met them again at the top station. Dani found the ascent to the hut very difficult. He felt tired and couldn't get any food down, which was rather unfortunate—I had to make a huge sacrifice by eating his portion as well as my own. I was ravenous and could have eaten a horse. It was important to eat and drink regularly to hasten recovery. Röbi and I had a very entertaining evening in the hut. As often before, we ended up in the kitchen and chatted until the early morning hours.

Dani did not recover during the night, and he stayed in the hut the next morning while Röbi and I climbed up toward the Windjoch Col. From here Röbi continued directly to the Nadelhorn, while I climbed the Nadelgrat ridge to scale the Dürrenhorn and then traversed across to the snowy ridge to scale the Hohberghorn and Stecknadelhorn. Three summits: now that's what I call Swiss efficiency! Röbi was waiting for me on top of the Nadelhorn. I climbed up and down a bit before I continued up the rocky ridge toward the summit of the Lenzspitze so he could get photographs. It was covered in fresh snow, which made finding tracks impossible. A roped party of two came down from the Lenzspitze, so that I did not have to break trail the whole time. In the middle of the snow-covered ridge we met and thanked each other for breaking trail. I did not stay long on top of the Lenzspitze, my fifth summit of the day. After taking the obligatory selfie as well as a summit video, I continued my traverse of the Mischabel Range.

In the meantime, Röbi had descended to the hut and had hopped into a helicopter to take some aerial photographs. From the Lenzspitze I traversed across to the Dome. This section was pretty exhausting since I kept breaking through the crust. On the summit I could finally see the ridge leading to the Täschhorn, which would be the most challenging section of the day's traverse. It looked demanding and somewhat menacing. It was steep and covered in heaps of snow, which was pretty wet at this time of day. My euphoria from having done six summits in a day was dampened. I started to descend, and it took ages. I was dealing with brittle rock covered by about 20 centimeters of soft snow. It did not feel right, but I still continued for a bit, hoping that it would get easier after I was past the lowest point of the ridge.

I hadn't gotten there yet, however. I tried to find the best way by stopping after each downward move and carefully checking where to put my feet next. Several times I was forced to step into the flank. This was a nightmare since there was no grip in the snow, and I couldn't tell whether the rock underneath was solid or loose. Finally I sat down to consider where to continue. Right below me the rock was vertical, and it did not seem to be climbable on either side of the ridge. I pulled out the route description. At this very moment the helicopter with Röbi in it came toward me. What unfortunate timing! Me sitting on the ridge and looking at the route description was not the best picture. But I didn't get too stressed about it and finally found out that I had to keep left to get down. This was not fun at all. I gave it a go, but the wet snow and rocks immediately began to crumble beneath me, and I turned back. I tried again a little farther to the right but only moved down for 2 meters before I returned again. I looked around. The route definitely went down there, but it was certainly no terrain to down-climb without a rope. It was far too dangerous.

I climbed back up toward the Dome. Ascending was definitely easier and safer. I gave Röbi, who was still hovering above me, a sign, but he did not understand what I meant. He flew to the bivouac at the Mischabel on the other side of the Täschhorn. We were going to meet there and climb the Allalinhorn as well as the Alphubel and continue to the Britannia Hut. When I reached the top of the Dome for the second time, I called Röbi to tell him that I wouldn't be able to make it. He was lucky, since the helicopter was still there and could take him back. From the top of the Dome I started the long way down to Randa. Sitting in Randa and waiting for Dani and Röbi, it suddenly dawned on me that Patrick Berhault had fallen to his death from exactly that ridge I'd just been on. That had been during *his* attempt to climb all eighty-two 4000-meter peaks. This realization sent a shiver down my spine, and I was glad to have abandoned the climb.

How should I continue? I had no other choice than to ride my bike back to Saas-Fee the following day, go to the Britannia Hut, and scale the mountains from the other side. Dario, the manager of the hut, looked after us splendidly, and the evening continued into the late hours of the night. This sort of socializing might have slightly compromised my climbing the following day, but social contacts were an essential part of the project. From the outset the primary goals of the project were to climb and have fun.

In the morning I skied up the Strahlhorn. It seemed to take an eternity to get up the slightly ascending glacier, and the summit just did not want to come closer. The ski descent made up for it, though: it took only about ten minutes. I then climbed up the Hohlaub ridge to reach the summit of the Allalinhorn. I could have also summited the Rimpfischhorn on the way, but I wanted to save it for Nicole. She was going to join me that afternoon, and we wanted to climb the Rimpfischhorn together the following day. As was often the case, Dani was waiting for me on the summit. His reliability was a great support, and we simply had a wonderful time together during the whole project.

We descended via the normal route, and I quickly bagged the summit of the Alphubel before I walked to the train station to collect Nicole. Back at the Britannia Hut Dario welcomed us with delicious refreshments, including white wine, cheese, and the local beetroot sausage. A wonderful eve of a ski touring day with Nicole! The following morning we skied up to the Rimpfischhorn. It was already the end of June, and I had never been on my skis so late in the year. The scrambling on the summit ridge was a welcome add-on, and shortly afterward we were sitting on the highest point, which was pretty crowded. We quickly took in the view and started to head down since we wanted to avoid snow that had gotten too soft. In such perfect spring conditions, even I enjoy skiing. On the ascent the snow had been frozen, but on the way back down it was soft and fun to ski. When we got back to the Britannia Hut, it was so hot that I changed into shorts. We each grabbed a deck chair and treated ourselves to a traditional Valais platter of dried meats, sausage, cheese, pickles, and rye bread.

Leaving this pleasant place nestled between the gigantic glaciers was not easy. However, my next goals were beckoning in Zermatt. As I was too lazy to put my trousers back on, I skied to the cable car station in my shorts. Nicole grabbed my skis and took the cable car down to the valley, while I ran down to Saas-Fee. We met again at the parking lot, where Dani had already settled in for the afternoon. Nicole went home, and I pedaled to Randa, where I met Dani at the campsite.

The following morning my legs were feeling heavy, and not even a second cup of coffee would wake them up. I needed some stretching exercises to make things better. Around noon I got on my bike and cycled to Zermatt. I met Andi Steindl in a pizzeria to discuss the plan for the following days. I had not met Andi before. He is a close friend of Simon Anthamatten, to whom I had initially reached out. Simon, busy guiding and completing his helicopter pilot training, had suggested contacting Andi, and I had been convinced that a friend of Simon's would be a friend of mine. Andi works as a mountain guide and skiing instructor but is also a trained carpenter, just like me. And he was extremely fit! He had climbed the Matterhorn from

Zermatt in an amazing two hours and fifty-seven minutes. I doubt that I would be able to do that! We talked about the Monte Rosa region, which, unlike me, Andi knew very well. He was convinced that we should be able to climb all the summits of the Monte Rosa range in a single day. I loved this plan!

From Rotenboden we ran to the new Monte Rosa Hut. Dani took the train up to Rotenboden and joined us later. When we approached the hut, a futuristic building with an aluminum shell in the shape of a crystal, I was mightily impressed. What I saw had nothing in common with a classic Swiss Alpine Club hut. The hut is equipped with state-of-the-art energy-efficiency technology. It has photovoltaic power plus a heat recovery system and a cogeneration unit. Its beautiful woodwork made my carpenter's heart skip a beat.

It was another short night. We started at 1:00 a.m., with Andi setting a fast pace. I was looking forward to the day, but I was a bit worried that I wouldn't be able to keep up. It was pitch black, with a new moon, and I could barely see anything, but with Andi doing the routefinding I could just follow him. A cold wind was blowing at the Silbersattel Col, so we each put on another layer before climbing the ridge to the summit of the Nordend. We then returned to the saddle, and soon afterward we reached the top of Dufortspitze, Switzerland's highest mountain. It was still dark. We traversed across to the top of Grenzsattel. It was just starting to get light when we reached the top of Zumsteinspitze. A red sky bathed the surrounding peaks in a magical light. At sunrise we reached the Capanna Margherita Hut, which is the highest hut in the Alps and is on the way to Signalkuppe. We stopped here for breakfast. The hut was full of climbers who had just gotten out of their bunks and were looking at us, puzzled. *Where have those two guys just come from so early in the morning?* they must have wondered. After coffee and a piece of cake, we filled our water bottles and each bought a Coke for later.

Reenergized, we continued our tour and climbed the Parrotspitze, Ludwigshöhe, and Vincent Pyramid. At times I wasn't even sure which summit we had reached, but I completely enjoyed the moment and the feeling of moving efficiently. We left our backpacks on top of the Vincent Pyramid and quickly went over to Punta Giordina, the only summit in the Monte Rosa range that lies entirely in Italy. We descended to the Lisjoch and traversed the Liskamm from east to west. Slowly we were getting into terrain that I knew a lot better. We summited the twin peaks Castor and Pollux. The snow was still hard and stable, and we were making good progress. Our goal was getting closer.

Half-running and half-sliding, we descended from Pollux. The only tour left was the traverse of the Breithorn, a route that is usually heavily trodden since it is near the Little Matterhorn cable car station and often used by mountain guides and their groups. But there were no tracks that day! The sun had softened the snow, and we broke through it and unexpectedly had to struggle. Our heart rates were up and our legs were tired when we finally reached the summit. From the Breithorn it was just a stone's throw over to the Little Matterhorn station, where we had a few well-deserved cold beers. It had taken fourteen hours and eighteen minutes to climb twelve summits.

We stayed the night at the hut next to the cable car station to be close to the starting point for our next goal, the Matterhorn. Running down to Trockener Steg was a cruel start since our legs were aching from the efforts of the previous day. We reached the Hirli via Furggsee and carried on to the Hörnli Hut, where we took a short break to eat and drink. From there I was hot on Andi's heels. After I found out that he had climbed the Matterhorn's Hörnli Ridge something like seventy times, I happily let him lead.

It was warm enough for us to run in our T-shirts. Once at the Solvay Hut we changed from running shoes into mountaineering boots, and we reached the summit two hours and fifteen minutes after we had set out. Considering that Andi had done it from Zermatt in two hours and fifty-seven minutes, our time was not particularly fast. Still in our T-shirts, we sat on the rock, enjoying some food and drink. We saw only two other roped parties up here, making it pretty quiet in Matterhorn terms.

Back at the Hörnli Hut we spoiled ourselves with a big portion of rösti topped with fried eggs. I still had to run down to the valley, while Andi had the luxury of taking the cable car from Schwarzsee Lake. I had spent two unforgettable and perfect days with him. When you have to make so many decisions, it is important to understand each other without exchanging many words. It does not always work so harmoniously.

The time had come to go back to the Täschhorn. Dani accompanied me to the Täsch Hut, and I then summited the Alphubel for a second time and continued to the Mischabel bivouac. Being on my own, I considered this route the safest since it did not require a glacier crossing. The ridge from the Mischabel bivouac to the Täschhorn was not as long as the ridge coming down from the Dome, but it was likewise brittle and full of loose rock. In the evening I was relieved to have added this piece to the puzzle since it had been weighing on me. I still had to go back to the Bernese Oberland to finish the unclimbed summits there, but otherwise I was on track.

The following day I met Andi Wälchli in Randa to climb the Dent d'Hérens with him. I was looking forward to touring with him again. It had been a long time. We used to climb together a lot, but now he had a family, and his life was a bit more settled than mine. Andi really identified with the project and even cycled from Randa to Zermatt with me. On the long approach march to the Schönbühl Hut, we had a lot of time to talk. While the hut was jam-packed in the evening, leaving us with little space to move during dinner, we were more or less alone on our way to the Dent d'Hérens in the morning. This route is hardly ever climbed these days, and I knew why when we had to climb underneath a gigantic serac for quite some time. I hoped that this enormous ice tower was not up to anything stupid that day.

I really enjoyed the climbing. It started off with an ice wall, then flattened out somewhat before we had to negotiate a steep ice gully. We could see the lights of headlamps along the ridge above us. These must have been the climbers coming from the other side. The day was slowly dawning. It was fabulous to be here with Andi. It was just like in the old days; we were just a little older. Before Andi went back to the valley after our climb, we shared a plate of dried meats. I felt sad that our time had come to an end. I would have liked to climb some more with him, but I was on my own again. The next goal was the Dent de Blanche, which I also climbed from the Schönbühl Hut.

Right after that I jogged up to the Arben bivouac. I was sure that I would be on my own up there and was looking forward to the solitude. In the space in front of the bivouac, I did some stretching exercises and let the sun shine on my face. Sometime later I saw some people moving toward me. What a shame! I wouldn't be on my own after all. Not long after this the guy in the lead greeted me: "Morning, Ueltsch!" I could not make out who it was at first, but it must be someone I knew—only a handful of people called me Ueltsch. As it turned out, it was Reto Schild with a client. What a coincidence! Reto and I had been on Denali in Alaska together, and we had later shared some climbs in Nepal. I was increasingly convinced that the eighty-two summits project had been one of the best ideas of my life. I had met so many friends I had not seen for a long time and who shared my passion for the mountains. Reto was now working as a full-time guide to feed his family. We spent the whole afternoon talking and discussed the question of risk. Reto told me that he had been very lucky the previous year when the rope on which he had been rappelling broke. This was unusual: with today's technology, ropes pretty much only break when they are cut by a sharp edge during a fall. But still, it happened to him. We had to accept that there would never be zero risk in the mountains, no matter how careful we are.

The route via the Arben ridge to the Obergabelhorn was very pleasant, and it was almost a shame that it was not longer. Just before 8:00 a.m. I reached the Rothorn Hut, where I had arranged to meet Dan Patitucci. He was going to climb the Zinalrothorn with me. In the hut I was served real coffee and an apple. After days of instant coffee this felt like heaven! When Dan reached the hut I gave him some time to rest. He used to be a bike racer and was still training every day, so he was pretty fit. We took our time since I wanted to give Dan a chance to take photographs. There was no reason to hurry. The only thing I did not want to miss out on was the cake in the hut; I wanted to be there before it was all eaten up.

After the climb we would have had enough time to descend all the way to the valley, but as Dan's wife, Janine, had come up to meet us, we spent a pleasant evening together. The hut had just opened for the season so we were spoiled with fresh vegetables that had been delivered by helicopter.

Now the moment had come to return to the Bernese Oberland and complete the missing summits. If I stayed here for the Weisshorn–Bishorn traverse, I would have to descend to Zinal, and that would take me even farther from the Bernese Alps.

▲ ▲ ▲

After a few intense climbing days I had to bike the long stretch from Randa to Fiesch. I was supposed to meet Nicole there and climb the Fiescherhörner and the Finsteraarhorn with her. I had gotten used to biking, and I no longer minded the heat. On the contrary, I liked feeling the sweat running down my body. There was always enough water on the bike, so dehydration was never an issue.

Dani was already waiting for me at the parking lot of the Fiescheralp cable car. While Nicole and I climbed together, he could go home for a few days and have a rest. Before Nicole arrived I quickly went back to the village to buy some ice cream. I had been looking forward to that ice cream since riding the last kilometers into Fiesch. Nicole arrived at 3:00 p.m. She picked up the luggage and took the cable car while I walked up. At the beginning my legs felt heavy, which was not surprising since I had biked a long distance that morning. I was starting to feel the cumulative effect of the last few weeks. There had not been a day when I did not do any physical exercise. After about five minutes, however, the feeling of heaviness seemed to disappear. My view narrowed, and I just ran. The only thing I saw was the path disappearing. This was a great feeling, something triggered only when I exerted myself. On slower runs I could never focus like this since too many disturbing thoughts would enter my brain.

Nicole was already at the Fiescheralp when I got there. After a good dinner and comfortable night at the hotel, we ascended to the Finsteraarhorn Hut via the Aletsch Glacier and the Grünhornlücke. Up until that day I had only descended the biggest glaciers in the Alps, not ascended them. When we were young, Markus Iff and I once came down the Mönch via the Aletsch Glacier just to save money. We were both the proud owners of a Swiss rail card, which was valid for the stretch from Fiesch to Fiescheralp but not for the trip from the Jungfraujoch. That descent had been a lot longer than the ascent via the North Face of the Mönch.

While we were walking across the glacier, I could hardly wait for our lunch break since I had made myself a delicious sandwich, a welcome change from my usual energy bars. Finally, at Concordia Place, we unpacked our picnic and marveled at the impressive ice landscape around us. This is where the glacial streams of Grüneggfirn, Ewigschneefeld, Jungfraufirn, and Grossem Aletschfirn merge into the Aletsch Glacier. I could see why masses of people came here from the Jungfraujoch to look at this magnificent natural spectacle. We veered off to the right, climbed the Grünhornlücke via the Grüneggfirn, descended to the Fiescher Glacier, and traversed across to the Finsteraarhorn Hut.

Climbing with Nicole means a lot to me. I enjoy sharing these unique experiences with her. But I always have to control myself and make sure I am not going too fast. Generally I tend to expect other mountaineers to be at my level and then get surprised that they are not as fast as I am. With Nicole though, I have learned how to address this situation. She has improved significantly over the past few years and is now very sure-footed. We either move on a rope together, or I put her on a short rope. For the descents we have come up with our own system. Long descents leading over hard snow have become quite difficult for her since she had to have her foot surgically stiffened as a result of a climbing accident. The solution is for her to slide down on her bottom and then for me to stop her on the rope. It is the trousers that suffer most from this technique. Fortunately we do not have to do this very often.

We set off early the following day, not because the ascent of the Finsteraarhorn would take such a long time but because I planned to also tackle the Grosse Grünhorn afterward. The track was easy to walk on. An icy wind had picked up so we stopped for a while at the Hugisattel to add layers. We continued on the ridge without crampons since we could easily circumvent the few icy sections. Climbing on rock with crampons is always a pain. The foot bends at a greater angle, and climbing is generally more strenuous than it is without them. Once on the top of the Finsteraarhorn, we sat down in front of the cross with its inscription *Soli deo honor* ("Only for God's honor"). We had reached the highest point of the Bernese Alps in brilliant weather and were completely on our own. We had passed a roped party, and they had not arrived yet. When we got back to the hut, I had enough time to climb the Grünhorn while Nicole was enjoying the afternoon sun on the terrace.

When we walked up the Fiescher Glacier toward the Fiescherhörner the following day, I was surprised by its sheer size. It was almost as massive as a Himalaya glacier. Nicole and I climbed to the Fiescher Col, from which we first scaled the Hintere Fiescherhorn and then the Grosse Fiescherhorn. We then crossed the Walcher ridge and reached the Mönchsjoch and the Jungfraujoch from there. After a good cup of coffee in the restaurant, Nicole and I went our separate ways. She took the train down to the valley while I continued my mission. Before starting I quickly called the Hollandia Hut to find out whether they had any spaces for the night. I told them that I was still at the Jungfraujoch and would get there in the late afternoon.

The hut warden was skeptical and doubted that I would make it. I assured her that distances were relative and that she should not worry.

Well-fed and full of energy, I stepped onto the glacier from the Jungfraujoch station. I was happy to follow the tracks of the glacier trekking groups since walking alone across a glacier was not my favorite pastime. I had gotten used to inspecting the terrain very closely and avoided any dangerous-looking sections. At Concordia Place the glacier was rather dry, revealing the crevasses. However, a little farther on it was soft and wet, and I had to pick my route carefully to avoid the big crevasses there.

I arrived at the Hollandia Hut just over two hours after leaving the Jungfraujoch. When the hut warden saw me, she said: "Ah, it's you! I was convinced that the guy who called would not make it here in time, so I didn't prepare any dinner for you." She did offer me a piece of homemade cake, though, which I devoured, along with a cup of coffee, before I fell into bed.

After I'd had a closer look at the Aletschhorn, I abandoned my plan of climbing it via the Haslerrippe. It had been very warm and dry, and the rib looked loose and brittle. I decided to go from the Lötschenlücke to the Sattelhorn the following morning and traverse the whole ridge to the Aletschhorn. It only took me an hour and fifty minutes to reach the summit from the hut, which made it a relatively short day out. I then descended and made my way across the Long Glacier to the Lötschental Valley. The glacier certainly lived up to its name. It dragged on forever, and it took me quite some time to reach the pastures at the Fafleralp. However, I still got there before Dani, who was going to bring my bike. I looked for a comfortable spot and had a rest. Nicole and I got married at the Fafleralp in 2008. This place was full of beautiful memories, and I didn't mind at all that I had to linger for a while.

▲ ▲ ▲

When Dani arrived I immediately hopped on the bike and headed to Randa, planning to reach the Weisshorn Hut that day. What a diverse day! First climbing, then biking, followed by running.

Unfortunately the weather was unsettled the next morning. Shortly after I left the hut, it started to snow. It was July 13, and even though it was a Monday—not Friday the thirteenth—I briefly wondered whether this would be the day to have a rest. *Nah*, I thought and abandoned the superstition instantly. The east ridge leading to the Weisshorn was easy to climb, and ascending its north ridge across to the Bishorn was straightforward. I could not really get lost there.

When I reached the summit of the Weisshorn, I was engulfed by thick fog and it was snowing. But by now I had gotten used to the bad visibility and did not for a minute entertain the idea of going back to the Weisshorn Hut. I started traversing the north ridge. The climbing was getting more demanding. The rocks were covered in a sheet of ice, requiring me to put on my crampons. I did not mind being challenged, but it bothered me that my left eye kept freezing shut. The wind blew from my left side, and the falling snow was pretty wet. Whenever my eye froze shut, I had to pull it open again, hoping that I would have some eyelashes left at the end.

The spiky ridge looked rather terrifying when it suddenly emerged from the mist. The rock was covered in ice and snow. The atmosphere felt eerie, especially since I was climbing this ridge completely on my own in the snow and fog. The ridge was pretty well protected, though. I found many bolts where I could secure myself and, if need be, I could use them to rappel from. I rappelled only two pitches at a section where the route dropped vertically into a notch. I had taken a 20-meter length of 5-millimeter rope as well as a 2.4-millimeter paragliding rope. At the belay point I tied the ropes together and threaded them through a carabiner. I used only the thicker rope for my rappels and the thin paragliding cord for pulling the rope down. This technique was a bit cumbersome, but it was efficient and fast. Every time I come up with a system like this, I feel like a child, and when it actually works I am proud of myself.

I knew I had reached the top of the Bishorn only because of the summit sign; visibility was about a meter. I could not see a thing, but I had no choice. I still had to descend to the Tracuit Hut. Climbing via the normal route, the Bishorn is considered one of the easiest 4000-meter peaks in the Alps, and I was convinced that I would find a good broken trail leading down to the hut. However, nobody had been up here in such bad weather, and I did not see a single track. I took my smartphone and marked my position. The app of Swiss Maps worked like a fully functioning GPS. It is amazing what smartphones can do.

Due to the low visibility I wanted to avoid walking across the glacier, and so I headed toward the rocky crest. I'd rather do some climbing than fall into a crevasse! But I was not sure whether this ridge would lead me to the glacier plateau. After a few minutes descending I took out my phone to double-check whether I was on the right ridge. But there was nothing to check: my phone had switched itself off. Shit! Why now? The battery had been fully charged. On all the other climbs I had put a battery pack into my pocket just in case, but this time I had been sure that the battery power would last, so I had not taken one.

Stupid, but there you are. I stuffed the phone right next to my chest in the hope it would warm up and come back to life again, and then I continued. I was sure I was on the right ridge. Well, pretty sure. If I wasn't on the right ridge, then I would just have to climb up again.

I could cope relatively well with such situations. I had been there many times before. In the worst case, I would have to bivouac somewhere. The weather forecast was better for the following day, so I would be able to find my descent route. Yes, it would be a cold night, but I had slept without a sleeping bag at 7000 meters. Admittedly it was very cold, but I knew that it was not life-threatening. My past experience gave me a certain peace of mind. Coming down the ridge was actually quite easy, and as the fog was slowly lifting I got a better idea of where I was. I stopped to check my phone, and it now had enough juice for me to find my position on the GPS. Yes! I was on the right ridge. The only obstacle that remained was the steep barrier that lay between where I stood and the glacier plateau, which I had spotted on the map.

I continued to descend until I got out of the fog. Finally I could see my surroundings and realized that I could get down to the glacier without problems. Lower down I saw a few mountaineers. It was all clear again. Phew! This had been exciting, but adventures like these are what define mountaineering for me. Weather and conditions vary, so the experience is always different. The traverse from the Weisshorn to the Bishorn had been pretty challenging that day, but it would have been a different story in fair weather. It always depends on the conditions and on the abilities, experience, and physical condition of the climber. Had I already been tired on the Weisshorn, the traverse wouldn't have been that easy for me. Had I not had decades of practice, I would have reached my limits sooner. But as it happened, the tour turned out to be pleasant and exciting at the same time.

Dani was waiting for me at the Tracuit Hut. He had even carried up my paraglider. I was thrilled to see how well our small team was working. We were on the same wavelength. The wind was too strong to take off from the hut, but luckily we found a suitable place lower down. I felt a bit guilty since Dani had to slog down to the valley while I was comfortably flying down, so afterward I bought him a beer. I then jumped onto my bike and rolled down into the Rhone Valley. I was very happy that there were no uphill sections on this ride. We stayed at a campsite in Sion and continued to the Grand Combin the following day.

Now I was back to being a cyclist again. I started quite early in the day, hoping to have a tailwind in the morning. Slowly but surely I got the feeling that everything was running smoothly. My average speed was between 37 and 39 kilometers per hour. For a lone rider unable to take advantage of drafting, this speed was pretty impressive. Heading toward Martigny, I slowed down significantly on the uphill section to Bourg Saint-Pierre. I was glad when I finally got there and Dani and I could start our hike to the Valsorey Hut, where we arrived just in time for dinner. After the meal we helped with the dishes, got stuck chatting in the kitchen, and enjoyed drinking homemade Génépi liqueur.

I was pleased that Dani had decided to join me to climb the three summits of the Grand Combin the following day. We reached the summits of the Combin de Valsorey and Combin de Grafeneire pretty quickly. When we finally stood on top of the Combin de la Tsessette, I suddenly realized that I had just reached the last Swiss 4000-meter summit. Even if something unexpected happened now, I had summited all 4000-meter peaks in Switzerland. The French Alps were next in line. In order to celebrate this achievement, I suggested to Dani that we continue to Chamonix and have a burger and local beer in my favorite restaurant there. Dani loved the idea, and so did I—even though it meant cycling over a few passes on the way.

▲ ▲ ▲

We set up at a campsite owned by a man from whom Nicole and I had rented a studio in Chamonix the previous winter. I really appreciate knowing the people around me. It makes me feel more comfortable and more at home. Dani and I were ahead of schedule, which meant I had to wait for two days for my next partner, German mountaineer David Göttler, to arrive. Two rest days would do no harm, but I couldn't sit still—the weather was too nice. I took my paraglider and ran up to the starting ramp at the middle station of the Brévent. The thermal was not great, and I did not get very high, but I could still fly to my heart's content. After a while my harness got uncomfortable, and I landed in the valley.

David and I had planned to climb Les Droites, Aiguille Verte, Grande Rocheuse, and Aiguille du Jardin. The weather did not look promising, though. We started early in the morning toward Montenvers and walked across the glacier to the Couvercle Hut. The normal route of the Les Droites turned out to be brittle and not really gratifying. The weather was deteriorating, and I hoped that we would be spared a thunderstorm. On the summit ridge David asked me to stand up on a rocky pillar since he wanted to take a photograph of me from below. My hair was standing on end, and the air was charged. The things you do for a good photo! We then descended pretty quickly and reached the hut without getting caught in the storm. I was thrilled that David and I had gotten along so well and that everything had gone smoothly despite the less than optimal conditions. Having passed the hardship test, we started planning a Himalaya expedition for the following spring.

On the second day we climbed the Moine Ridge on the Aiguille Verte, traversed via the Grande Rocheuse to the Aiguille du Jardin, and returned via the same route. At the Montenvers station David took the train while I continued on foot, as usual. This time, however, the train was significantly slower. When David arrived in Chamonix I had already showered and was enjoying a cold non-alcoholic beer in front of the tent. Running definitely has its benefits! The next day David went back to Spain to be with his girlfriend, and Ueli Bühler and Röbi Bösch arrived. Ueli had been my partner in one of my first Himalaya expeditions, on the West Face of Pumori. The four of us, including Dani, intended to climb Mont Blanc du Tacul via the Devil's Ridge.

The starting point for this tour, the Refugio Torino, was actually easy to reach since the cable car line ends right in front of it. For me it was more complicated, though. From Chamonix it was probably best to climb the Frendo Pillar to the Aiguille de Midi and then cross the glacier to the hut. My friends took the cable car up the Aiguille de Midi, where they waited for me. Ueli and Dani took another cable car across the Glacier de Géant, while Röbi came to the Aiguille de Midi Hut with me. This way I did not have to cross the glacier on my own. I started off in running shoes and changed into my mountaineering boots later. A thunderstorm that had raged here the previous day had left the lower part of the Frendo Pillar pretty wet, and the granite, which was overgrown with lichen, was especially slippery. I slowed down.

It was dry higher up, and I enjoyed climbing on good rock. The crux was a section of Grade V climbing. I had climbed the Frendo Pillar a few times before, and it is definitely a rewarding ascent with a very convenient finish. From there you can get straight into the cable car and go down again. That was not my intention this time, however. At the exit point I had two choices: to either go right or left of the rock. The left side looked good. It was still covered in snow, while the right side was covered in shiny blue ice. At this very moment Röbi called and asked me whether I would come up from the right side. He said he was still up on the Aiguille de Midi and wanted to take a few pictures. I did him the favor but not without uttering a curse or two as I struggled on the ice.

In the Rifugio Torino we met Dutch climber Martijn Seuren. Martijn had contacted me earlier to ask me whether he could join me on the traverse of the Grandes-Jorasses. He told me he had climbed almost all 4000-meter peaks in the Alps and that the only one missing was this traverse. This would make him the first Dutch national to have climbed all 4000-meter peaks. I liked this challenge and after having thought about it, agreed to climb the Grandes Jorasses with him. I had not met him before, but if he had already climbed eighty-one of the 4000-meter peaks, he had to have good technical skills and experience. He had arrived at the hut a day earlier in order to acclimatize.

First Ueli, Röbi, Dani, and I climbed the Devil's Ridge. Once on the glacier we waited for the day to break since we did not want to miss the starting point of the climb. With the first sunbeams of the day, Dani and I stepped onto the ridge: a perfect moment in extraordinary light. The red glow illuminating the granite was exactly as in classic photos of the Mont Blanc massive. When Ueli and Röbi joined us shortly afterward, the light was still magical, and Röbi used the moment to take some photos. He planned to take photos on this climb, which meant we had to be patient and allow him to take his time.

The Devil's Ridge offers classic granite climbing, Grades IV and V. Including the main summit, the ridge has five 4000-meter peaks. This would definitely be a taxing day, with a lot of ups and downs: climb to one summit, rappel back down to the lowest point, and start up again to reach the next summit. This was basically what we were doing all day. It took a long time. We got stuck behind two relatively slow climbers, but unfortunately we were not quite fast enough to overtake them. The other problem was that they also inhibited Röbi's photography, which meant that we sometimes had to wait to make sure that they were well away and out of the picture.

At the last tower I left my friends to their own devices. It was already late, and I wanted to reach the summit of Mont Maudit the same day. From the last tower of the Devil's Ridge, I continued without a rope and would meet my climbing partners back at the hut. As soloing was a lot quicker, I reached Mont Blanc du Tacul in no time and quickly continued to Mont Maudit. From there I descended via the same route and met Dani, Röbi, and Ueli, who were on their way to the Aiguille de Midi to catch the cable car to the Rifugio Torino. I jogged back to the hut via the glacier.

I met Martijn at the refuge, and we discussed the plan for the following day. We left it open whether we would climb the Aiguille de Rochefort and the Grandes Jorasses in a single day or whether we would sleep at the Canzio bivouac. It was impossible for me to judge how fast Martijn would be. We took a stove and some provisions, just in case. Ulrich Karrer, a South Tyrolean who was working on the construction of the new cable car, also wanted to join us as far as the Aiguille de Rochefort. He would have to be back at the hut at 7:00 a.m. to start work. The plan was for Ulrich and Martijn to go directly to the Rochefort ridge while I did a short detour to the Dent du Géant before catching up with them.

In the morning the three of us left the hut together. Ulrich showed me the starting point to the Dent du Géant, and I set off at my usual pace. After all, I had one more mountain to climb than the others. The first pitch was slabby. After about 50 meters of climbing, I reached a big fixed rope that led all the way to the summit. It took me about twenty minutes to reach the top, from which I could see Ulrich and Martin's headlamps moving up the Rochefort ridge. I started to descend. The last 50 meters I had to down-climb, which felt a bit uncomfortable since it was still dark, and the rock was slippery and had no good holds. Once on the bottom of the rocky section, I put on my crampons and ran to the Rochefort ridge.

Suddenly I saw one light move toward me. Was it that late already? Was Ulrich already going back to work?

I was right that it was Ulrich. He looked somber and said, "Not good at all!" At that moment I saw a light far down on the north side. I immediately put two and two together, and Ulrich confirmed my worst fears. Martijn had taken a fall. Ulrich had already informed the hut.

I looked down. Should I climb down to Martijn? The flank looked icy, and I only had one ice axe. The light did not move. I looked up to get an idea of how far he must have fallen. A long way. In fact, too far to have survived.

My phone rang. It was the PGHM (Peloton de Gendarmerie de Haute Montagne) rescue team of Chamonix. I knew many of the mountain rescuers, who were mostly passionate mountaineers and climbers. Someone had mentioned my name during a conversation, and they wanted to know whether I had any more information. I explained the situation to them. Martijn had tumbled down at least 300 meters. The rescuers were getting ready and would leave as soon as day broke. I was waiting at the accident site to instruct the helicopter pilot.

As always, it seemed an eternity before the helicopter came roaring through the darkness. Martijn had fallen into the bergschrund, which made the recovery complicated and time-consuming. In the meantime, Ulrich and I were put on the long line of the helicopter and taken down to the helipad in Chamonix. We needed to get Martijn's personal details to get in touch with his relatives. I only knew his name and that he worked at the Bächli outdoor shop in Bern. In the meantime, Martijn's body was recovered from the ice and brought down to Chamonix. I identified him.

A sad day. Why did Martijn have to die? What happened? I could only guess that even though he was wearing crampons, he must have slipped on an icy section during the descent. Of course, I wondered whether he had been rushing and whether he had felt pressured to move fast because he was climbing with me. I had told him several times to go at his own pace. Contacting me and asking to join me on this climb had been his own decision and responsibility. But I couldn't help feeling somewhat guilty.

I decided to put the project on hold, and Dani and I went home. I felt the need to find Martijn's family and talk to them. The rescue team was not allowed to give us the family's contact details, but at nine o'clock that evening I had finally found their phone number, and I called them. Martijn's father spoke a little German, and Nicole's father, who is Dutch, helped me with the conversation. It was a difficult call, but at least it gave me the opportunity to explain to them what had happened.

It took me a few days to decide whether I should continue with my eighty-two summits project. Would this reflect a lack of respect toward the deceased? Martijn's accident had shocked me and struck me deeply, even though I hadn't really known him and had not been with him when it happened. The accident had also affected Nicole, who worried that it could be me one day. We talked a lot about it.

At the end of the week, though, I knew that I wanted to continue. Martijn was dead whether I stayed at home or finished the project. His death would also not stop me climbing outside the eighty-two summits project. For Martijn's family the loss was tragic and inconceivable, but life went on. We mourn, but the world keeps on turning. Our time will come. Without exception, we all will meet our end.

▲ ▲ ▲

Dani and I went back to Chamonix. This time I was allowed to take the cable car up to the Rifugio Torino. This had been where my project was interrupted, and this is where I wanted to continue. I walked down to the Val Veny on the Italian side to meet Jonathan Griffith and tackle the 4000-meter peaks south of Mont Blanc. We descended to the Eccles bivouac together. Martijn's accident made it somehow difficult to simply continue where I had left off. I found it hard to be completely carefree again. Lost in thoughts, I put one foot in front of the other. It could be me one day. There was no guarantee that I wouldn't make a mistake, slip, and fall. That this wouldn't be the end. I was happy to have Jon at my side. It was important to have a close friend around at times like this.

To make matters worse, it was raining when we started. We waited for a while at the Monzino Hut to see how the weather would develop. Finally the rain eased off, and we were able to continue, but the dry spell did not last for long. At least the rain had turned into snow. We grumbled but continued. In Scotland it would be normal to set out in weather like this; in Chamonix it would be stupid. When we reached the Eccles bivouac, we were wet to the bone. It snowed so hard that we decided to spend the following day in the bivouac. The huge amount of fresh snow had increased the avalanche danger significantly. The following day we hung out at the bivouac in brilliant sunshine. On the one hand it was annoying, but on the other hand it gave the mountain a chance to clear the snow. All around us we heard the thundering of avalanches tumbling down into the valley. In the bivouac we sat completely alone right in the middle of the glacier. The south side of Mont Blanc is pretty remote. The approach routes are long and demanding and require full commitment. Abandoning a climb for whatever reason often requires a huge effort. This inconvenience makes the Italian side less popular than the French side, where access is a lot easier.

In the afternoon we broke trail up to the couloir, which we were going to climb to get to the Frêney Glacier the next morning. Jon had just returned from an expedition in Pakistan, and instead of resting he had immediately joined me to climb in the Mont Blanc region. I had sent him a message asking him whether he would like to join me on a few climbs, and he had promptly accepted while he was still at the airport. He was incredibly motivated. In Pakistan he had been on his seventh attempt to scale Link Sar, a 7000-meter peak. This time, he and Andy Houseman had managed to open a new route to the west summit, a great success. He had many interesting stories to tell, which made the waiting periods much more bearable.

In the morning we followed our tracks up to the Col Eccles, rappelled to the Frêney Glacier to reach the Col de Peuterey, and climbed the Aiguille Blanche de Peuterey. It was still dark when we climbed the four pitches leading up to the northeast summit, from which we descended and traversed across to the main summit just as the sun was coming up. Jon made the most of the beautiful morning light to take photos and video on the ridge before we returned to the Col de Peutery.

My next goal was the Pilier d'Angle. Its summit is not very prominent, just a pointy spike on the ridge, so I climbed the whole ridge, not wanting to risk missing the highest point. Jon waited on the saddle, taking pictures of me as I approached.

In the most pristine snow conditions, we climbed the Peuterey ridge, first to Mont Blanc de Courmayeur and then to the summit of Mont Blanc, where we met a couple of Italian mountain guides doing some filming for a TV series. We quickly continued since we still had a long day ahead of us. After our descent via the Dôme du Goûter, Jon went directly toward the Gonella Hut while I did another lap to the Aiguille de Bionnassay. We reunited at the bottom of the glacier, where we roped up and ascended to the Gonella Hut. Here we had our first proper rest and a huge plate of pasta. The film crew had also just arrived and offered us a helicopter lift down to the valley. I declined but told Jon to take the opportunity to get down quickly. He said he would rather slog across the endless moraine with me. What a friend!

The following day Jon went back to Chamonix, and I flew to the Netherlands from Geneva to attend Martijn's funeral. It was a very emotional day. When I saw his family and friends pay their last respects to him, it became clear to me what it meant to lose someone close to you. And how final death was. In previous years I had lost a lot of friends or acquaintances in the mountains, and I had literally seen a few people die, but I was not prepared to give up mountaineering. It was my life, after all. Yet the funeral made me think about how far to go in the future and how to weigh my projects against their risks.

In the evening Dani picked me up in Geneva, and we went back to the campsite in Val Veny. The ascent of the Brouillard Pillar was next on the agenda, in two days' time. Matteo Pellin, the mountain guide who was managing the campsite with his brother Luca, supported the project. He wanted to know when I expected to get to the Monzino Hut. I calculated my time and came up with 5:30 a.m. A while later he told me that he had just called the hut warden and that breakfast would be waiting for me.

I got up at 4:00 a.m., had something to drink, and ate a piece of bread before I headed out. I reached the Monzino Hut on time, and, as promised, breakfast was ready. The friendly hut warden went outside with me and showed me the bottom of the ridge. I crossed the glacier at the hut's level and reached the place where I had to turn off to get onto the ridge. The shiny new bolts indicated that this new and better route had just been opened. I climbed along the ridge, which was covered with a lot of loose rock. Given that I was completely on my own up there, it would not have put anyone in danger if I had kicked off some rocks. The route was long and impressive. First I reached the Aiguille Rouge du Brouillard, and then I climbed the two 4000-meter peaks Punta Baretti and Mont Brouillard before descending into the Col Émile Rey. I had reached the starting point for the Brouillard Pillar, which did not look inviting. It was relatively warm, with water running down the rock, and every once in a while a rock came flying past. I would have to be quick!

I started climbing. The steepest section is usually vertical ice, but it looked so hollow and brittle that I did not feel like hanging off it. I was convinced it would collapse so I looked for another solution. It seemed that I might be able to climb farther right across the rock. I traversed over, clipped both ice axes onto my harness, and used my hands for climbing. The granite was not really compact here either—it was a bit brittle. Before I trusted my weight to each handhold, I scrutinized it, and I kicked my feet hard against the rock to see whether footholds were safe.

After about 250 meters the slope eased off. The rest of the way to the Picco Luigi Amedeo did not pose any difficulties, although the rock remained loose. From the summit I continued across to Mont Blanc and descended the normal route via Mont Maudit and Mont Blanc du Tacul to the Rifugio Torino. Once at the hut I felt tired, which was not surprising after having covered 21 kilometers of distance and 4260 meters of climbing. So I wasn't too unhappy that the following day's climb would be rather short. I planned to descend to the Canzio bivouac and give the Grandes Jorasses another go.

I had to get up early because a thunderstorm was forecast. Dani had come to the hut; he wanted to climb the Dent de Géant. We climbed to the start of the route together, and I put him on belay until he reached the start of the fixed rope. He continued on his own and descended to the Rifugio Torino after his climb. I traversed via the Aiguille de Rochefort and the Dôme de Rochefort to the Canzio bivouac. I had been feeling uneasy the whole day. I kept on thinking about Martijn and was worried about Dani. I didn't usually worry about him, but I felt huge relief when I received his message that he had reached the hut.

I arrived at the bivouac before noon, which was a good thing since the sky was now overcast and fog had started to rise. Fortunately the thunderstorms never came, and there was no precipitation at all. This meant the rock would be dry the following day. I was reassured and felt more self-confident. I just had to get used to climbing on my own again. Dres Abegglen, a mountain guide I knew, and his client joined me at the bivouac, which made my stay up there more lively.

It was already light when I set out at 6:00 a.m., which was good for my morale. It took one or two pitches for my head to clear. After that everything went smoothly. I just climbed, and I climbed well! The sections on the Pointe Young were uniquely beautiful, exposed and steep. When I reached the top of the ridge, I heard the rattling of the chopper. Jon and I had arranged to meet up here to take photos and films, and the timing could not have been better. I kept on climbing, maintaining my rhythm. The razor-sharp ridge was really exposed, with steep vertical drops on each side. Some sections I traversed directly along the edge. I hung off the edge of the ridge with my hands while I pressed my feet against the steep rock face.

I had to move to the right, climb across a couloir, and get back onto the ridge to reach Pointe Margherita. The couloir was full of snow, but there were tracks, which spared me from putting on my crampons and saved some time. I was just using my two ice axes. Once on the top of Pointe Margherita, I felt the sun's warming rays on my skin. I had arranged for Jon to come up here and shoot a few photos, so I sat down and had something to eat and drink. After about twenty minutes, the camera team arrived in the chopper. Only then did I continue my climb.

I had regained confidence. I was neither stressed nor tense. I simply climbed like I had before and trusted that I knew my trade. I didn't worry about times or difficulties, but the descent was in the back of my mind. I wanted to reach the glacier while it was still frozen, which would reduce the danger of snow bridges collapsing and my falling into a crevasse. That was the only reason for me to make good time.

I climbed across Pointe Elena, Pointe Croz, and Pointe Whymper; from there, I could see two people descend from Pointe Walker, the main summit. They were pretty early! The tracks indicated that someone had bivouacked up here, and I guessed it must have been those two climbers. When I crossed over to Pointe Walker, the two came toward me. It was a tired-looking French couple. We had a brief chat, and they told me that they had been on the ridge for four days. They asked me how long I had taken to get to the Canzio bivouac. I looked at my watch and asked them whether they really wanted to know. They said yes. I had been on the go for two hours and twenty minutes.

Before they started their descent I gave them something to drink as well as two energy bars and showed them the route. I then tackled the last bit to get to Pointe Walker. I was relieved when I stepped on the last summit of the Mont Blanc massive. I had done the lion's share of my grand traverse, with only the Gran Paradiso and the Barre des Écrins left. Both mountains were technically easy, which meant that the weather would not be such a decisive factor. I stayed on the summit for a few more minutes and enjoyed this beautiful moment. It was still early and the glacier was in the shade.

I ran down to the couloir. The French couple had not gone very far, and I caught up with them quickly. They offered to descend with me so that I would not have to cross the glacier unroped, but I declined. It was still frozen, and at my speed I would be on the other side in about an hour. I gave them the rest of my food and carried on. I was back down before noon.

I felt somewhat liberated. There was not much that could go wrong now. On the other hand, I almost felt sentimental knowing that my eighty-two summits project was coming to an end. I wanted to make a conscious effort to absolutely enjoy the last two summits. Back at the campsite I welcomed the friendly and familiar atmosphere. Matteo congratulated me with a beer. After a shower I rested and chatted with Dani in front of the tent. We would leave the next morning, and the thought made me feel a bit melancholic. I would have liked to stay.

In the evening Matteo and Luca had a surprise for me. They had organized a celebratory dinner with polenta, cheese, dried meats, and a delicious dessert. A few bottles of champagne were cracked open, and the campsite management team and some other guests celebrated with us. It was wonderful. Dani had put together a few photos, which he projected on a big screen. Reviewing the project this way inspired memories for me, and it was interesting to see how it all began.

In the course of the evening, I talked with two Spaniards, Óscar Pérez and Carles Rossell. Both are passionate trail runners and come here every year for training. Carles told me that he was organizing a race in the Pyrenees at the end of October, stretching over 70 kilometers and with 6700 meters of altitude, including some easy rock climbing. I would have loved to take part! The previous year Óscar had run up all 3000-meter peaks in the Pyrenees, which also sounded very appealing. As they both had brought bicycles, they wanted to join me on the ride to Valsavarenche the following day. I liked the idea since it would be a welcome change to bike in a team of three, my only worry being that I might not be able to keep up with them. When I lay in my sleeping bag late that night, I felt tired but too emotionally excited to fall asleep. Too many impressions and ideas were whirling around in my head. There were so many ideas and projects to do in life!

With all the good-byes, it took quite a while to get away the next morning. Carles and Óscar waited on their bikes for ages. Finally it was time to go. We biked at a speed that allowed us to chat, and the ride to Pont was still done in no time. The village was situated in an appealing valley, and the surrounding hills were much gentler than the rugged Mont Blanc massif, with its sharp needles and uneven glaciers. The terrain was a lot less steep and rough. Given the number of people milling around in the streets, it seemed to be a popular tourist destination. Dani and Res Aeschlimann arrived shortly after us. Res and I used to share a flat in Gsteigwiler, which seemed ages ago. This was a great chance to do something together again. The three of us, including Dani, would scale the Gran Paradiso together. We bid farewell to Óscar and Carles.

I set the pace on the way to the hut. When Dani is in front he usually sets off far too quickly but then runs out of steam later on. I moved more slowly than usual to give Res a chance to keep up. The hut was packed, and it would be interesting to see how all these people would fit on top of the Gran Paradiso, which is not very big.

By the time we got up at 4:00 a.m., the route was already crowded. We took our time having breakfast and then leisurely started our ascent. The chain of headlamps in front of us seemed endless, and I was not sure whether they were all on the right path. Unfortunately Dani felt sick and turned back after about forty-five minutes. Res did a great job, and we managed to reach the summit before the masses. Only one mountain guide and his client were up there with us. It was peaceful, there were no crowds, and there was plenty of space on the summit. From the Madonna statue Res and I climbed across to the main summit, which involved a short appel and a climb of about five minutes along the ridge. It was even more peaceful up here!

On the descent we met a lot of teams heading up. One and a half hours later we were back at the hut enjoying a cappuccino. Now only the Barre des Écrins beckoned.

▲ ▲ ▲

I had one longish bike trip ahead of me. I had to get to Ailefroide, the starting point for the Barre des Écrins in the Dauphiné. It is the most southern and most western 4000-meter peak in the Alps. My friend Heinz Heer had offered to accompany me on this tour. Dani would pick him up in Aosta, and then we would meet somewhere on the way. From Pont I rolled down to the Aosta Valley, which was great fun. However, before I knew it, the road went uphill again. The Little Saint Bernhard Pass turned out to be longer than I had expected. I had anticipated that being called "little," this pass would be shorter than the Big Saint Bernhard, which I had been on during an earlier trip. I was completely wrong. My afternoon stage became longer and longer, and the heat did not help. After 96 kilometers I stopped in a hotel in Bourg Saint-Maurice and called Heinz to ask him to meet me there.

The following morning we biked to Val d'Isère and the Col l'Iseran. We took it easy and cycled at a moderate speed so we could talk. Once we were at the bottom of the pass, I started to pedal hard, and then I waited for Heinz on top of the pass. When he got there he'd had enough and got into the van. I continued on my own. After about 120 kilometers I stopped in Saint-Michel de Maurienne, where I got caught in a thunderstorm. It poured and spoiled my fun.

I had planned to cross the Col de Galibier and exceed the 200-kilometer mark, but this downpour changed my mind.

This was France's cycling mecca, where you find the most difficult passes of the Tour de France. I now had the biking bug. The next morning Heinz started out an hour ahead of me. The roads were filled with cyclists, despite the rain. Incredible! I wanted to reach my limit and gave it everything. It went pretty well. Just below the pass I overtook Heinz, who was still looking pretty fresh. Dani was waiting for us on the pass. I ate and drank and then continued. Till then it had just been drizzling, but now it was pouring. I began to shiver and got cramps everywhere. This was impossible! I should have listened to Dani, who had told me to put on more clothes. Now I belatedly realized he was right. I had to stop. My hands were cramping, and I could barely use my brakes. I grabbed my phone with my stiff hands and called Dani to tell him that I urgently needed more clothes. He was still on the pass waiting for Heinz but said he'd be there immediately.

Shivering all over, I continued very slowly and stopped at the first restaurant. I was so cold that I had to go inside. I thought that the sudden presence of a drowned rat might irritate the restaurant owner, but I was completely wrong. A big group of cyclists sat at a table, each of them wearing a distinctive white bathrobe. I had not even finished an envious thought before I was handed just such a robe and asked what I wanted to drink. Shortly afterward Dani arrived with my dry clothes. After I had changed, I was good to continue all the way to Briançon. In the evening I felt satisfied having experienced such an intense day. I even felt sorry that the next day would be my last for biking. The stretch to Ailefroide turned out to be easy and pleasant, which was a nice way to finish.

On the other hand, I had to fight hard for the last summit. On August 11 I set off from Ailefroide at 4:18 a.m. It was pitch dark. Dani was waiting for me at the parking lot at the end of the road. I stopped for a drink, and he told me that the route continued behind the house there. After a quick handshake I carried on, running on a wide trail. As with every climb over the past two months, I felt excited. I was motivated to climb and immediately found my rhythm. After a while I encountered a big rock with a sign pointing to the Glacier Blanc and the Glacier Noir. I was headed to the Glacier Blanc and was convinced that the arrow was pointing left, and so I went left.

In the light of my headlamp I could see the route. It first went around a few bends, then across a moraine with no path but lots of cairns to mark the route. I started to have doubts about whether I was actually on the right track, but the sign had been pretty obvious. By the time I reached the end of the valley, though, I was sure that I had gone wrong. I took my phone out of my backpack and a glance at the digital map confirmed that I had ended up on the wrong side of the mountain. My loud yell echoed through the whole valley, and then, not wanting to lose any more time, I started running back in the direction from which I'd just come.

I had been on the go for three hours and forty minutes when I got back to the valley floor and started from scratch again. I had to laugh at myself and at my warm-up run. What the heck, it was only another 2200 meters of altitude from here to the summit. And now it was light and I could see the way, which was actually not that hard to find.

Despite the long detour my legs felt fine. I ran like I had been running every day for the past two months. I had hardly any gear: just a pair of light aluminum crampons, one ice axe, something to eat and drink, long pants, and a jacket. Most of the climbers I saw were already coming down the Dôme de Neige. The tracks on the glacier were pretty good and enabled me to ascend quickly. I reached the top of the Dôme de Neige in shorts, which made me smirk. Climbing a 4000-meter peak in shorts and running shoes was not how you did it by the book.

The traverse across to the Barre des Écrins looked wild from where I was standing. Some clouds had gathered on the summit by now, so I put on my long pants and ran back to the saddle. There were no tracks up the Barre des Écrins. I guess most people were happy with having reached the Dôme de Neige. I put on my crampons and climbed the snow-covered ridge on its sharp edge.

Finally I stood on top of my last summit. Alone. On the one hand, I was over the moon that I had completed this big project successfully. On the other, I was sad that it was over. The past two months had been filled with intense experiences and encounters. I'd had the chance to spend valuable days with good friends, and countless wonderful moments had reminded me of how beautiful and unique mountaineering is. That my original partner had left the project near the beginning turned out to be a blessing in disguise.

I was also lucky that the summer of 2015 did not have any prolonged bad weather. Summers like this do not happen very often. And I couldn't have done it without Dani's support. His heart was in the project as much as mine was. He was passionate and motivated, and he was invaluable.

Of course, I am pleased about my performance. In sixty-two days, I had climbed 117,489 meters of altitude and covered a distance of 1772 kilometers. This was not a record, as some media called it. The Italian climbers Diego Giovannini and Franco Nicolini had climbed the eighty-two 4000-meter peaks in sixty days. If I deduct the week I stopped after Martijn's accident as well as the two waiting days in Chamonix, it would be less, but that is not what it was about. I had consciously taken my time for the climbs I did with Nicole. My eighty-two summits project was more about the journey than about numbers. And it inspired me to do more of what I love doing and not worry about what the public or the media say.

EIGER
THE FASCINATION
OF SPEED

In the autumn of 2015 I was in pretty good shape after the traverse of the 4000-meter peaks. My expedition to Nuptse in Nepal was due to start in the second half of September. I intended to scale the South Face of Nuptse with the North American climber Colin Haley, who is eight years my junior. Colin lives in Seattle but spends a lot of time in El Chaltén in Argentina. He is a real expert in climbing steep mixed faces in Patagonia and Alaska.

With its 7861 meters, Nuptse is directly opposite Mount Everest and Lhotse and is part of the Horseshoe made up by these three summits. We were not planning to open a new route but to repeat Valery Babanov's route. Originally from Russia, Valery had immigrated to Chamonix. In 2003 he opened a new line on the southeast buttress to reach Nuptse's east summit with his countryman Yuri Koshelenko. It took him three attempts to finish this line on the South Face, where several other accomplished climbers had failed. Since the face is very steep and extremely demanding technically, the pair set up four high camps and fixed ropes on the toughest sections. They reached the summit on a beautiful full moon night.

Valery and Yuri earned a Piolet d'Or for their incredible feat. Several mountaineers have attempted to climb this route in alpine style, which means climbing in one go from bottom to top without fixing rope or setting up high camps. Whenever I bumped into Valery in Chamonix, we talked about Nuptse. This kindled my fire. I always wondered why difficult routes in the Himalaya are so rarely repeated. Everyone hunts for a first ascent. Maybe this is because the media is much more interested in firsts. However, the fact that a route has never been climbed does not really say anything about its quality or technical difficulties. In my view repeating a route can be very interesting and exciting. You can reenact what climbers in the past accomplished and get a better feel for the technical difficulties. Most first ascents in the Himalaya were done in expedition style, and if you attempt to climb one of the routes in alpine style you will find plenty of opportunities to do something new.

The pre-expedition days in Kathmandu were not as carefree as usual that fall. The effects of the earthquake that shook Nepal in April 2015 were still visible. Most of the collapsed houses had not yet been reconstructed. In the earthquake 700,000 buildings collapsed, almost 9000 people were killed, two million lost their homes, and roads were cut off. The country found it hard to deal with this challenge. It became obvious what a desolate state Nepal had been in even before the disaster. The earthquake also had an impact on mountaineering in the Himalaya. In an avalanche in the aftermath of the quake, eighteen people had died on Everest alone, and all climbing was stopped on both the Tibetan and Nepalese sides of the mountain. Due to the ensuing humanitarian crisis and the chaotic situation in the country, not many trekking tourists came in the fall, which meant that Nepal had lost one of its biggest sources of income. This was precisely the time when Nepal *needed* tourists to come and bring money to the devastated country.

The situation was exacerbated by a blockade that crippled trade with India and led to acute shortages of gasoline, food, medicine, and building materials. An ethnic minority group, the Madhesis, felt discriminated against in the new Nepalese constitution, which came into force in September 2015. To push for their rights, they enforced this blockade, which lasted for several months. We would feel its effects when we got back to Kathmandu at the end of October.

Colin had hardly any experience in climbing in the Himalaya. This was probably why he was slower at acclimatizing than I was. It usually takes around two weeks for the body to get adjusted to the higher altitude. During this time it makes sense to ascend slowly and sleep high, even though your body is not fully acclimatized. After we had trekked for five days, we climbed the 6120-meter Lobuje and spent two nights on the summit. On the first morning Colin experienced the first signs of altitude illness, and we quickly went down. I accompanied him to Dzongla, which lies at 4200 meters. He then continued down to Pheriche, and I ran back up to the top of Lobuje. After I had spent another night there, I descended to Dzongla but left the tent and some other gear on the summit for Colin, who needed to spend a second night at altitude.

I stayed a few nights in the lodge in Dzongla to wait for Colin, and Lobuje was the training ground for my daily sessions. The weather was perfect, and it was warm enough for me to run up Lobuje in running shoes and light clothing. My metabolism adapted more and more to the altitude and the physical exposure. I loved heading out of the lodge with no gear to simply run up and down the mountain. I did my last trip from Dzongla to the summit in a mere hour and forty-seven minutes, with the round trip taking me two hours and thirty-five minutes. I had reduced Lobuje from a two-day tour to a morning run. My rate of elevation gain was 700 meters per hour on the ascent, and my rate of elevation loss on the descent was 1800 meters per hour. I particularly loved the middle part of the climb. The steep granite slabs had the perfect incline for running without having to use hands. Coming down the slabs always required a bit of an effort. I had to run as fast as I could to avoid slipping. It almost felt like flying. I loved experiencing the pure movement and feeling how my legs were carrying me, day after day. This is what mountaineering is to me, moving with natural lightness.

The weather remained perfect, stable and warm. I was acclimatized and ready for Nuptse, but Colin was still down in Pheriche. I was growing impatient and hoped that the weather would not turn by the time Colin was acclimatized. I had to accept that there was always the chance of someone getting sick on such an expedition, that physical conditions on a given day were different for each climber, and that there was a general difference in performance. Teams had to work together. Colin and I got on very well, and I was happy to be climbing with him, but at that moment I felt extremely frustrated looking at the surrounding mountains that were in perfect condition.

I called Colin, who said that he felt better and wanted to come back up in the next couple of days. I was still eager to move, so I asked him whether he would mind if Tenji Sherpa and I quickly climbed the North Face of Cholatse. He told me to go, saying that it would be a shame if I did not make the most of the perfect weather and conditions.

Tenji, with whom I had climbed several times and who was the official guide on our expedition, was enthusiastic about Cholatse. He belonged to the young generation of Sherpas who go mountaineering of their own accord and actually enjoy it. For the older generation, mountaineering was mainly a source of income, just like it was in the Alps 150 years ago. Swiss mountain guides used to climb to earn money. Without the English, who hired mountain guides for their first ascents, many summits in the Alps would not have been climbed until much later. The Matterhorn is a prime example of this. Englishman Edward Whymper was the driving force in putting the first climbers on the summit, in 1865.

Mountaineering tourism is the main source of well-paid employment in Nepal, even though a lot of the profit ends up in the pockets of corrupt government officials in Kathmandu. Unlike climbing Sherpas, who work hard, liaison officers earn a good salary without really having to do much of anything. Sometimes they don't even go to base camp but stay in Kathmandu. They earn about two thousand dollars for signing a few pieces of paper and being present at the expedition briefing in Kathmandu before and after a climb. When they do join an expedition all the way to base camp, they are often a burden, just eating the food and not really contributing to the team. This discrepancy in salaries has increasingly led to friction among the Nepalis. Tenji had to work hard to achieve his income. But even though he still struggled to make a living, he was now in a position to do things for pleasure rather than just for money. And that's why he was here.

▲ ▲ ▲

At 6440 meters Cholatse is a beautiful summit towering 1800 meters above the small settlement of Dzongla. I had climbed its imposing, steep, and technically difficult North Face twice before. The 1400-meter face was a real challenge for Tenji, but he had practiced a lot over the summer. One of his Everest clients had invited him to climb in Germany and the Dolomites. Since he also went climbing in Nepal as often as time and money allowed, I was certain that he would be able to climb the face.

Together we sorted and packed our gear. Sherpas are used to carrying a lot, so I had to tell him repeatedly that we would go as light as possible and that we needed to be fast. I gave him one of my small backpacks to make sure that he would not fill his big one with unnecessary gear and food. We took only light sleeping bags, one mat, and food for one night on the mountain. I was sure we would reach the spot, just below the ridge, where Freddie Wilkinson and I had been forced to bivouac in bad weather in 2011. We could then decide whether to climb the French route or to attempt a direct line that had been on my mind for a long time.

When we left the lodge after coffee and pancakes, it was still pitch black and very warm. Straight out of the lodge, the path went down to a river. I was already thirsty and drank a little water from the creek before we climbed across the moraine to the bottom of the face. I consciously took the lead and set the pace. In my years of climbing in the Himalaya, I have noticed that Sherpas don't pace themselves. They usually set out at full speed, continue until they run out of steam, and then stop to rest before continuing on at full speed again. I do not like these intervals. I find them exhausting and need to move at a constant pace. Tenji had adapted to my rhythm, but sometimes he could not avoid falling back into his old pattern.

We put on our crampons at the bottom of the face. Once on steep terrain I observed Tenji's moves closely to gauge his technical climbing abilities. I was relieved to see that he was moving safely up the face, which was slowly illuminated by the light of the rising sun. It was still a long way to the summit, but the snow conditions were good, and we could climb calmly and smoothly. Every time I asked Tenji whether he was okay, he responded: "No problem!" Fortunately I knew him well enough to sense when things were not okay, even though he said "no problem." Over the years our relationship had changed and he was no longer my employee. We had become friends. As a guide, he knew exactly what to do on an expedition, but now we were a team, and this climb had nothing to do with work.

We climbed about halfway up the face without a rope. When we reached a rock barrier, we roped up, and I led a few pitches. I set up a belay point for Tenji to tie in and put me on the rope. I would lead, and once he had given out the full length of the rope, he would follow me. When putting in protection, I made sure to always have two fixed points between us. When I ran out of gear, Tenji came up to me and gave me all the gear he had taken out. This system allowed us to make good progress and be safely on a rope at all times.

Tenji had never climbed such a technically difficult face, and he was doing really well. We worked well together and were making good time. But in the end I decided to go for the French route since I deemed the direct line too difficult for Tenji. As the face got increasingly vertical, Tenji slowed down significantly. He was experienced in rock and ice climbing but had never used his skills on such steep faces. The ice on the direct line looked pretty brittle, and there were several vertical pitches to the summit. I would just have to come back to Cholatse another time to open this beautiful direct line.

Climbing from the face onto the ridge also had its difficulties. The terrain was a mix of snow, ice, and rock, and the climbing was steep and demanding, although probably less so than on the direct route. We were now climbing in the classic style, belaying one pitch after the other. There were not many places to put in gear, but this was my problem and not Tenji's. After two pitches we reached a balcony where we could stand and have a rest. We ate some chapatis with honey, a welcome change from energy bars. Tenji was obviously having fun. His eyes sparkled.

After about ten minutes I led the next pitch. It was full of snow, and I had to dig occasionally to find firm ground, which took some time. After another two pitches we reached the summit ridge. The sun was still up, there was hardly a breath of wind, and it was nice and warm. I was surprised to realize that we would actually reach the summit in one day. Now we were moving together again and indeed stepped onto the summit just before dusk. We did not stay up there for long, though, since we wanted to make the most of the remaining daylight to get as far down as possible. At about 6200 meters we found a good place for a bivouac. I gave Tenji the one sleeping mat we had and lay down on our two backpacks.

We did not have to start early the next day. There was no time pressure, and we waited for the sun to reach our bivouac and warm us. Little did we know that we had chosen the wrong spot. The sun's rays did not reach us but appeared about 10 meters below. There was nothing we could do but crawl out of our warm sleeping bags and move quickly. Once lower down, we could enjoy the warmth of the sun. We descended independently, at our own speeds, although every once in a while I waited for Tenji in order not to lose sight of him. We were back in the valley before noon.

We had descended to the south side of Cholatse, and the way back to Dzongla led us over the 5400-meter Cho La Pass. We had lunch at a lodge in Dragnag, just below the pass, and continued in the afternoon. We could feel how tired we were, and the ascent of the Cho La pass dragged on for a while. Fortunately there were not many people who could see how slowly we crawled up the pass. Back in Dzongla, even Tenji celebrated our ascent with a shandy (beer mixed with Sprite). He hardly ever drinks alcohol, which I find laudable since many Sherpas suffer from an alcohol problem. Compared to other Nepalis they earn a fair amount of money on expeditions and have a high reputation, but in the down times between expeditions they have little to do, and many hit the bottle. I don't drink much myself, but after achievements like this I think it is absolutely acceptable to have a beer. A bed and warm sleeping bag felt like heaven afterward. I fell asleep feeling both content and motivated and slept into the early morning hours.

▲ ▲ ▲

A few days after Tenji and I had come back from Cholatse, Colin was sufficiently acclimatized. He had spent another night on the summit of Lobuje and another one a little bit lower, at 5600 meters. Finally we were ready to go. But now the incredibly long weather window was about to close. I was hoping that this change in the weather would not mean the end of the season. The weather forecast looked so dismal that we decided to descend to Namche Bazaar. It was the best thing to do since the much lower altitude of 3000 meters allowed our bodies to recover. We enjoyed a couple of days in the village, and I could feel the energy pouring into my body. When we walked back up the hill on the third day, all the bakeries that had been closed before were now open. It was a real joy to indulge in all the different kinds of bread, cinnamon rolls, croissants, and cookies. There was also proper coffee available in the Khumbu now, which made me very happy.

We bumped into the French mountain guides, Hélias Millerioux and Benjamin Guigonnet, with whom we were sharing a permit. They also intended to open a new route on Nuptse. Two days later we arrived at our base camp in the settlement of Chukung. The weather window was definitely over. It had snowed, and the forecast predicted high winds. We had no choice but to wait and see what happened. However, waiting and seeing was not enough for me, and so I went running every day. It was the perfect training, and I absolutely loved it. Running here prevented me from returning home spent and unfit after a Himalaya expedition. I had come up with a new strategy for my expeditions. I would run and do excursions to higher altitudes on a daily basis, while I would sleep at moderate altitudes of between 4200 and 4500 meters. This was a good way of keeping, or even increasing, my performance level. I would only spend as many nights up high, which takes a huge toll on a body, as was necessary for acclimatization. The fact that I made the most of the waiting periods and even went bouldering on a big rock near Dzongla also had a positive impact on my attitude. The waiting days were not "lost" days, and that made me relax a bit. I did not have the urge to go out and start my expedition in bad weather just for the sake of doing something and not having to return home empty-handed. This way I was less inclined to go "have a look" in suboptimal conditions, exposing myself to dangerous situations.

When we were in Chukung the Spanish ultrarunner Kilian Jornet popped in to see us. He was on his way to Kuala Lumpur for a sponsor event and made a quick detour to the Everest region to train. On the spur of the moment he decided to join our training camp. We went running and climbing alternately, and the bad weather did not faze us. We were optimistic and had fun. At 6000 meters the weather was warm and calm, but at 7000 meters the winds were blowing hard, and above 8000 meters storms were raging. Big wind drifts were visible on the summits of Lhotse and Nuptse. The weather forecast continued to indicate high winds, between 80 and 100 kilometers per hour. Given the winds and heavy snowfall up high, there was no point in even trying.

Kilian, Hélias, and I climbed a beautiful ridge leading from the Amphu Laptsa Pass to a nameless peak of around 6200 meters. We did not take a lot of gear, the short climbing sections were easy, and I took great pleasure in being lightweight. From the summit we descended the other side down to Chukung. Kilian and I talked a lot about our speed climbs, and I was surprised to hear that he had never climbed the North Face of the Eiger. We arranged to tackle it together as soon as we were back in Europe if the conditions on the face were favorable for climbing it safely.

After Kilian left the weather forecast did not improve significantly. The jet stream had already moved far to the south, and we read on the internet that the Japanese climber Nobukazu Kuriki had abandoned his solo attempt on Everest a week earlier. I had given up hope of tackling a difficult route, but the three youngsters in my team were incredibly motivated. Being in the valley in brilliant weather makes it difficult to believe that the conditions on the mountain are not good enough for climbing. I was the oldest and most experienced and knew what I was talking about. Nevertheless, I still allowed the three to convince me to attempt an easier line, which was to the right of the English route that we had initially planned to climb. This was probably the only possibility for climbing Nuptse under the conditions.

I checked and compared different weather forecasts every day to find the best day to attempt the summit. I could have done without it, but I pulled myself together. Was I lacking the enthusiasm of the young people? Perhaps I just needed their zest, and then it would be possible. At least there were four of us to break trail.

Finally Hélias, Ben, Colin, and I set out on October 23 at the crack of dawn. We planned to reach 7000 meters on the first day and bivouac, then reach the summit the following day and return. For a mountaineer 2500 meters of altitude in a day sounded like a lot. For a runner, however, it was moderate, and after all, we had the whole day, and the terrain did not look too difficult. There were a few sections with an incline of about 65 or 70 degrees, but most of the face was between 35 and 50 degrees. When breaking trail, I was in my element. I found a good rhythm and was going at my speed. Just below the bivouac I waited for Colin and the two Frenchmen. At about 6900 meters we found a good spot, where three of us dug a platform while Ben was melting snow. As usual, Hélias was in a good mood and infected us with his cheerful spirit.

During the night a strong wind came up, and at 4:00 a.m., when we had intended to get going, it was clear that a summit attempt was out of the question. As soon as it got light, we had a bite to eat and descended. A lot of snow had fallen during the night, making the slope very avalanche-prone. Our tracks from the previous day had gone, and I found myself breaking trail again. I was moving very carefully and trying to see where most of the snow had been deposited and which direction the wind had been blowing from. Where were the snow pockets we needed to avoid? Where could we walk on a ridge with less snow? I concentrated but was slightly annoyed with myself for having gotten myself into such a tricky situation again. Early on I had told the others that I would not go if conditions were precarious. As none of them had ever been as high as 7000 meters, they were eager to reach this magical height, and I had tagged along. Why was it so difficult for me to say no? I was relieved when we were off the face and safely back down in the valley.

This marked the end of the Nuptse expedition, since even higher winds were forecast for the rest of the month, and November was usually too cold and windy for such high mountains. We decided to pull the plug and go home. I was still content with the expedition. I had spent an intense time with wonderful people, and I returned from the expedition in even better physical condition than when I had left.

▲ ▲ ▲

I did not have any professional engagements slotted for two weeks after I returned to the Bernese Oberland at the end of October. When I was on the plane, I decided to use those two weeks to prepare my presentations. But high pressure in the Alps made me change my plans. A two-week weather window was forecast, which was unusual for November. With such good conditions, there was no way I could sit in front of my computer.

I still had some unfinished business on the Eiger and wondered whether now was the time to finish it. In 1991 American rock and ice climber Jeff Lowe had soloed a route on the North Face, which had not been repeated since. During his attempt he had spent more than a week on the face and had to sit out two storms in a bivouac. It was a crazy feat of a possessed man who was running away from professional and private problems. His *Metanoia* was a rather mysterious route. There was no proper route description, and nobody really knew which line it actually followed. I wanted to follow Lowe's footsteps and uncover some alpine history. The tragedies he had encountered during his life also touched me. Once a legendary mountain climber, renowned for his athleticism and incomparable passion for the mountains, Jeff now suffers from an incurable neurodegenerative disorder, requires a wheelchair, and needs 24/7 care.

It was hard to tell what the conditions on the Eiger would be like at that time of year, and, rather than relying on blogs, I decided to have a look myself. Dani Mader, my faithful supporter during the eighty-two summits project, joined me. The left leg of the Spider—the central icefield on the North Face—seemed very long, which is always a reliable indicator of good conditions. On this same ice gully I had opened a new route in 2001, which I dubbed the *Young Spider*.

We took the first train to the Jungfraujoch and got off at Stollenloch, where we were hit by summer-like temperatures. It did not feel like November at all. At the first rock face we inspected the initial two pitches of *Metanoia* that I had climbed during a reconnaissance trip two years earlier. Back then I'd only had a day at my disposal and just wanted to check out the first two pitches. The whole route would not have been possible to climb anyway, as there was not enough ice. I took almost all day to climb those two pitches. They were very challenging, especially as there was hardly a place to put in a piece of safety gear. Jeff Lowe must have really been crazy! After having climbed the two pitches, I rappelled and left the ropes there for another attempt.

After having had another look at the steep cliff with Dani, I quickly abandoned my initial idea of soloing *Metanoia*. Most of the bolts I had put in two years earlier were now dangling on the rope. If they came out on their own, they would certainly not hold a fall. We discovered, however, that above the cliff the section between the Hinterstoisser Traverse and the Schwalbennest was icy enough to climb. The face was almost vertical and covered in frozen snow. We thought: *It should work!* Going via the Hinterstoisser the route avoids the traverse and goes directly up. In summer this line is impossible since the slabs leading up to the Schwalbennest have no holds whatsoever. A good layer of ice is needed.

After this reconnaissance I packed enough gear for three days. Nicolas Hojac, a young alpinist from Bern and a member of the junior squad of the Swiss Alpine Club, had agreed to join me. We circumvented the first cliff by climbing directly to the Hinterstoisser Traverse. The pitch from the traverse to the Schwalbennest turned out to be pretty committing. After about 3 meters I could place a cam into a crack, which was hidden under the snow. After that there was no place to put in protection. I had to pull myself together to climb the small overhang. The snow was pretty soft, and it was difficult to find a firm grip with my axes. The cam was now about 10 meters below me. Falling would certainly be painful! I climbed very carefully and felt relieved when I reached the Schwalbennest. Nicolas seconded the pitch, and once he was at the belay point we pulled the haul bag up to us.

From the Schwalbennest, *Metanoia* follows the classic Heckmair route all the way to the second icefield. Nicolas led this pitch, and I followed. On this section I was able to carry the haul bag on my back since the going was not so steep. Fortunately the snow was hard enough to climb safely. The haul bag was weighing on my shoulders, and my calves started to hurt since I was standing on my front points most of the time. Once we had crossed the second icefield, the route went straight up. We could make out a ramp from below and realized that it had to be the ramp leading to the prominent central band. We climbed the ramp pitch by pitch until we came across a bolt. Jeff Lowe certainly would not have used bolts. This could not be his route. But where was it?

We climbed following our instincts and reached the band in the evening. We were probably too far to the right, but Jeff's route description was so vague that it was difficult to tell which way he had taken. Up until now the climbing had been magnificent, and we had made good progress in perfect conditions. Now we would set up a bivouac and wait and see what the next day would bring. The bivouac was not as comfortable as I would have liked it to be. It was just big enough not to fall down. However, we were compensated with a spectacular view of the lights of the town of Grindelwald. We had enough food and warm sleeping bags, which we probably didn't need in these mild temperatures. The climb would definitely have been easier without the haul bag, which was far too heavy, got stuck on every ledge, and was simply annoying. It belonged to Dani, who had written his last name on it: Mader. We started calling the bag the Mean Mader.

The next morning we packed the Mean Mader again and continued. Nicolas and I were climbing in blocks and did not alternate the lead after every pitch. This saved us having to hand over the gear from leader to leader all the time. I took the lead first, and no matter how hard I tried to get away from that route, I kept on coming across bolts. This was definitely the Japanese route. Still, the climbing was pleasant and we continued to follow this line. The most awesome pitch was a wide, almost vertical crack. I could make out a bolt about 15 meters above us but could not see anything beyond that. I was hoping to find more bolts since we did not bring any cams big enough for this crack. The crack was easy to climb, but there were no more bolts, and it was a 50-meter pitch. Just below the next belay point I discovered another bolt, which I was very happy about since there were some tricky moves coming up. I was impressed by Nicolas, who came up carrying the Mean Mader.

Once you veer off the original line it is very hard to find the route again. I could not stop looking for *Metanoia*, but the rock on the Japanese route was incredibly solid, and we were moving beautifully together. In the end, we stayed on that route. We were making pretty good progress and expected to reach the west ridge that day. I led another few pitches before Nicolas took the lead for the last three combined pitches up to the ridge.

When we were on the west ridge, we had about an hour of daylight left. We started our descent immediately and were already below the icefall at dusk. From here it was only a stone's throw to the Eigergletscher station. At 9:30 p.m. we got back to Ringgenberg feeling very satisfied and joyful about the two days of sensational climbing we had just experienced.

▲▲▲

The same evening, a Thursday, I wrote to Kilian Jornet, telling him that the conditions on the Eiger were ideal. Kilian responded immediately: he would be free on Sunday. I was excited. My next adventure on the Eiger was just around the corner. I was fired up and full of energy. I hadn't enjoyed climbing like this for a long time.

On Friday and Saturday my training sessions were relatively easy. Kilian had suggested that we start our ascent of the Eiger from the valley. I had often considered this idea but never acted on it. After all, it added another 1400 meters to the climb. I was looking forward to climbing with Kilian, even though I was a bit apprehensive. Kilian's stamina was extraordinary. He had run 2050 meters to the top of the Matterhorn from the Italian resort of Cervinia in an hour and fifty-six minutes, and it took him only fifty-six minutes to get back down! When it came to running, he was in a different league. Over a distance of 50 kilometers, he was a whole hour faster than me.

On Saturday evening Kilian arrived in Ringgenberg from Chamonix. We packed two minimalist backpacks: sixteen quickdraws, two ice screws, and a 30-meter rope. Kilian took half a liter of water. Given that we were starting from all the way down in the valley, I decided on three-quarters of a liter. We also took one power bar and two energy gels each. We would wear running shoes and carry our mountaineering boots in our packs. We finished packing and turned in early.

After a quick breakfast we drove to Grindelwald Grund and then started running at a leisurely pace. I had to preserve my energy, and Kilian was pretty cool about adapting to my speed, though he could have run a lot faster. He did not see this as a competition or a race, and we ran at a pace that allowed us to chat. This was just a warm-up for him. He had told me that he was able to run 50 kilometers daily over an extended period of time. In training for a race, over two months, his daily runs entailed elevation gains of 3000 meters. Even I found this hard to imagine.

The path leading from Brandegg to Alpiglen was free of snow and easy to run on. Just below the start of the climb, we changed into our mountaineering boots. This made our backpacks significantly lighter. We encountered a good track on the lower part of the face and reached the Stollenloch in no time. The terrain was right up Kilian's alley, more running than climbing. I had to work hard to avoid being overtaken by him. Just above the Stollenloch the terrain got steeper, and we roped up. Since we wanted to move as efficiently as possible, we did not pitch the climb but moved together. I made sure that there were always two fixed points between us. It all went smoothly, and Kilian climbed very safely. We did not communicate much, but we both enjoyed the fast progress we were making.

Having climbed the face forty times, I knew it like the back of my hand and could split it into three sections. In an effort to save gear, I only clipped through the necessary bolts. This way Kilian only had to climb up to me three times to hand over the gear he had retrieved. Apart from that, we never stopped. Moving so quickly was great fun. The temperatures were still very comfortable, and the ice was solid and safe wherever we went. Kilian turned out to be an accomplished climber, but to be on the safe side, I belayed him on the most difficult sections. If you move on a rope together like we did, a fall of the second climber could be fatal since the leader would be dragged down as well. Once Kilian had negotiated the critical section, we continued to move on the rope together.

Despite our efficient system we still took a little longer than five and a half hours to climb the face. I concluded that Kilian was unable to use his speed on technically difficult ground. This made sense since he was a runner and not a climber, and he was climbing the Eiger North Face for the first time. We definitely made up for lost time on the descent, though. We ran down the west ridge all the way back to Grindelwald in two hours and twenty minutes and even managed to talk as we went. Going from the parking lot to the top and back had taken us almost exactly ten hours. I was not even tired—it just felt like a good day's training. I also liked the purity and simplicity of our climb. No public transport, no organization, just running.

My day with Kilian was extremely inspiring. While I had for quite some time been thinking of climbing the Eiger North Face all the way from the valley, I had never dared to do. It was a mental block. I had always thought that 3000 meters of elevation gain in a day was too much or that it could only be done on a perfect day. But for an ultrarunner like Kilian, this was completely normal, and he had never even entertained the idea of taking the train. I had to find out for myself that it was possible, which shows that only experience can break down barriers. Progress can only be made when you change your perception. I constantly went through this process in different fields—in running, in climbing, and in my professional life. With intense training, some things that have always seemed impossible suddenly become possible. Life is a never-ending learning curve.

▲ ▲ ▲

Being determined to make things possible, I was back at the bottom of the Eiger North Face three days later, on Wednesday, November 11. Once again I was with Nicolas Hojac. We were intending to do an even faster ascent as a roped team. He might not have had the endurance of Kilian or me, but he had alpine experience and a good feeling for the terrain, and he knew the face. This time we took the train to the Eigergletscher station. Nicolas was not confident enough to do the whole route from bottom to top. There were some good tracks on the Heckmair route, indicating that it must have been climbed a few days earlier. I took the lead since I had just had a lot of practice moving on a rope with Kilian. We climbed fast, benefitting from my having ascended the route a couple of days earlier, but we were under no pressure. I knew where the handholds and footholds were and remembered exactly where I had put in protection gear. It felt like home: everything seemed so familiar. On the icy sections, the existing tracks were very helpful. The brittle ice had been hacked away, and there were even footholds and handholds in the ice. Everything went smoothly, and once again climbing was a real pleasure.

After three hours and forty-six minutes we reached the summit. This was even faster than my first speed record of the Eiger North Face, and it was the fastest-ever ascent of a roped party. We had broken the record of Roger Schäli and Simon Gietl by thirty-nine minutes. Nicolas was amazed when he realized how fast we'd been. I guess he had just broken down a barrier.

▲ ▲ ▲

On Thursday and Friday I had a sponsor engagement in Grenoble. We discussed product development, but my mind could not quite focus on that. I was distracted by the thought of making the most of the brilliant weather and climbing the Eiger North Face again, solo. Gripped by this idea, I drove home on Friday.

The next morning I talked with Nicole about it. She was not happy with me making another solo attempt, but I did not want to miss this chance. I knew I had the ability to do it, and it was difficult to abandon the idea. It was like owning a Maserati that had to be taken out of the garage every once in a while, just because it felt good driving it. Living life as my own ruler is very important to me. Doing what I want to, deciding for myself, being in control of myself: these are the moments when I feel most competent and totally believe in myself.

I am not afraid to climb solo. I would not do it otherwise. Climbing without a rope has always been part of mountaineering for me. I grew up climbing easy routes without a rope, and on the occasions when we used a rope, we would not always use an Italian hitch. We would simply sling the rope around our shoulders. Nicole cannot quite understand this, since nowadays rock climbing is a totally different sport. You learn at the climbing wall, where it is paramount to properly belay the person climbing. However, it is impossible to protect every single meter on alpine tours— you have to rely on your own and your partners' abilities.

I tried to get Nicole to understand that in such pristine conditions the Eiger was relatively easy and safe. I would take a sling in case the conditions had deteriorated over the past three days and some ice had broken off on the route. Apart from that I wasn't planning to do a free climb. I would use some of the bolts to haul myself up. This would make the route a lot safer. But no matter how hard I tried, my arguments did not convince her. Even though Nicole had climbed the Heckmair route herself, it was hard for her to gauge in what spheres I would be moving up there and how much risk I would actually be taking. In her view, I was simply going without a rope, which meant that the worst could happen.

I completely understand that such situations are not easy for Nicole, and even though our relationship means the world to me, she sometimes gets the feeling that climbing is more important to me than she is. For sure, there are moments when I get carried away and am unstoppable. I yearn for these experiences in the mountains; they are a big part of me. If I deny this part of me, I'll wither like a spent flower. This is the only way I can also enjoy the times when life is calmer. I need both: the phases complement each other.

We continued the discussion on Sunday night, just before Nicole had to go back to Bern to start her workweek. She was still opposed to me soloing the Eiger North Face. But I went regardless. I had no choice. Once again the Eiger had put a spell on me. However, I had set a few clear parameters. I would not allow myself to ascend too quickly and lose control.

On Tuesday, November 17, I took the second train to the Eigergletscher station. I took my time getting to the bottom of the face in order to prepare myself mentally. Once there I changed from running shoes to light ice-climbing boots with fixed crampons. This combination saved a lot of weight and would allow for more direct climbing than the traditional mountaineering boots and crampons. I was convinced that these boots would work on the Eiger North Face.

As usual, I began my climb at the memorial plaques. Just before I started, I pressed the start button on my stopwatch and locked it to make sure that it would not stop accidentally. As there was hardly any snow on the lower part, I had to zigzag and could not take the direct line, which is only possible in deep snow. Now I just needed to find the right line. After only twenty-four minutes I reached the Stollenloch. Wow, these boots were fast! The Schwierige Riss [Difficult Crack] turned out to be half as difficult as expected. My movements felt completely firm and smooth, and with the light boots I encountered less resistance.

After about 50 meters on steep ground, I was back on the snow, and from here I traversed diagonally up to the Hinterstoisser Traverse. Unlike I'd done in 2008, I used the fixed rope to cross the slabs. I then climbed the dihedral to the Schwalbennest and crossed over to the first icefield.

Just below the ice gully I met two Spaniards who wanted to have their picture taken with me. I quickly joined them for the photo and carried on immediately. A lot of the ice in the gully had already been chipped away. At times I did not even have to hammer my ice axes deep into the ice. It was sufficient to place their tips into the small holes. This technique was efficient and got me to the second icefield very rapidly. The track leading up to the Bügeleisen was heavily trodden, almost like a path. My heart rate was still moderate. I was certainly not exhausted.

From experience I knew that the traverse to the Bügeleisen could be a bit precarious. This time it was covered in a thick layer of ice, which meant that I didn't have to clamber across the sloping rock but could climb across using my ice axes and crampons. I carefully placed my axes and the spikes of my crampons into the ice. I did not even stop at the Death Bivouac, where I usually took a short break and had a bite to eat. I had brought only gels, which I could also consume while climbing if needed. I used a hydration pack for water and had taken exactly half a liter. Since I had climbed this route with Kilian, I knew that this was sufficient. With the hydration pack I could drink without stopping and never lose my rhythm.

From the Death Bivouac I had to negotiate a small snowfield to get to the ramp, which could be arduous to climb in deep snow. This time, however, the ramp was covered in hard snow, which made for easy climbing. The waterfall chimney, the steepest section on the face, was also covered in a nice sheet of ice. I could clearly see the tracks of all the roped parties that had come up here over the past few days. The thin, brittle ice had been chipped away, leaving solid ice. The traverse from the chimney into the reclining gully turned out to be easy. I only had to swing my ice axe once to place it firmly into the ice. I pulled myself up, let my feet follow, and there I was, standing on top of the waterfall chimney.

The next 10 meters can be rather awkward in winter since it often gets a lot of snow deposit. It is not quite vertical, just steep enough to engage ice axes and not just rely on your feet. In soft snow it can be quite difficult to find a firm grip with your axes. This time around, the snow was hard, and the rock was covered in a perfect sheet of snow and ice. Climbing left around the corner was no problem, since I could place my ice axes firmly with one single swing.

I climbed over the Brüchige Band to reach the bottom of the Brüchigen Riss, where I overtook another roped party. The two climbers asked me how long I had been on the go. I had no clue and looked at my watch, which is something I hardly ever do. I was surprised to see that I had only been going for a bit more than an hour and a half. I had been climbing a lot more quickly than I'd thought, although it had not felt very strenuous. This motivated me to speed up.

The Brüchige Riss is the most exposed section on the Eiger North Face. I climbed the steep cliff on the side, with a sheer overhanging drop below me leading straight down to the second icefield. It was better not to look down that far, just far enough to check out footholds. For me this pitch is the most beautiful section of the entire face. The rock seems made to be climbed, and the handholds and footholds are big and beautiful and seem to be exactly where you want them.

I climbed across the Traverse of the Gods to the Spider, which leads to the top of the ridge. Such a demanding wall becomes quite easy when you have climbed it several times and are familiar with it. I felt completely at ease. It was not at all cold. I quickly climbed the cracks leading to the ridge before I reached the platform. From here I traversed across to the right to get to the last snowfield before the exit point. When I met another roped party it became clear to me why so much snow and ice had fallen on me while climbing the exit cracks. I had wrongly assumed that wind on the ridge was blowing snow into the cracks. I said hello and continued. The sun was just rising. The track on Mittelegi Ridge was heavily trodden, and I broke into a jog.

On the summit my watch indicated two hours, twenty-two minutes, and fifty seconds. I had not expected to be that fast, but I was very excited to have regained my record. The six minutes under Dani Arnold's time were not really ground-breaking. Such a performance depends on conditions on the face, and it is difficult to compare times. What was much more significant was my time difference compared to 2008, when it had taken me two hours and forty-seven minutes. I had free climbed the entire face without using a single bolt or fixed rope. On top of that, there had not been a single track on the face, which had made the effort greater this time.

What this indicated was progress. I had never found myself in a risky situation, and everything had been calculated and controlled. My speed had been moderate, and my heart rate had never exceeded 165 beats per minute. In 2008 my average heart rate for the climbs had been 190! This ascent had been absolutely safe. I knew that I had more potential still—and that I'd been able to control myself and had not gone too far.

After a short break I climbed down via the west ridge. The winter conditions made the descent much easier than in the summer, when you have to negotiate sloping rock. I was back at the Eigergletscher station within an hour. The next train wasn't due for half an hour, so I continued walking down to the valley. This gave me time to let things sink in and to reflect on my two weeks on the Eiger. That fortnight had not only been a wonderful end to the climbing season, it had also given me the opportunity to learn more about myself. The climb with Kilian had motivated me to increase my endurance or at least try to increase it. At my age my potential no longer seemed limitless, but I was convinced that climbers could learn a lot from ultrarunners.

While I ran down Alpiglen to Brandeegg, dodging all the hikers, I thought about what German mountaineer Reinhard Karl wrote in his book *Erlebnis Berg: Zeit zum Atmen* (*Adventure Mountain: Time to Breathe*): "The top was more than just a summit. There were myriad paths leading back down to the valley. After every up, I was a different person down." Suddenly all my experiences of the past two years, good and bad, came together in my head. I was no longer the same person who had raced up the Eiger North Face in 2008. I realized that I no longer wanted to exhaust my potential. I never wanted to revisit the zone I'd experienced on the South Face of Annapurna. At the same time, I knew that I could climb such a face at a risk that was acceptable to me. I could go a bit slower, climb with a partner, set up a bivouac, or just climb a shorter face. The most important thing was to stay aware of the risk at any given moment and control it. If I managed to do this, I would certainly be able to experience more exciting and beautiful moments in the mountains without killing myself.

AFTERWORD

"There are dreams which are worth a certain amount of risk."

—Ueli Steck

Climbing mountains has much to teach us. There are no official competitions, no medals, and no prize money, and to many it seems selfish, unproductive, and impractical. Climbers are conquistadors of the useless, to use the title of French alpinist Lionel Terray's memoirs. But among the many beauties of alpinism is its ability to transform a person.

Ueli Steck was one such transformed human, one of the rare ones who temper themselves in the forge of climbing at the highest level, incredibly motivated, who give much, sometimes their lives. He was visionary, and in testing and retesting himself he discovered and rediscovered himself— over and over. Through determination and effort, he became a person who knew himself—pride and humility alike.

People say that Ueli was gifted, that his ability was innate. But I believe that is completely wrong. Achieving his level of mastery in climbing is the result of long-term commitment that requires vision and consistency. That achievement is itself worth studying. Ueli envisioned what could be accomplished by a tremendously fit, technically excellent climber, and then he made himself into the personification of that vision.

He understood the connection between his vision for climbing big mountains and what he did with his life every single day. This is what most people don't understand about Ueli. The way to achieve one's dreams is by working constantly to bring them about. His ability to focus on and examine the relationship between alpinism and daily life is not only honorable, it is something to emulate.

Alpinism is not a sport of adrenaline, measured in seconds and fractions of seconds. Training takes years, expeditions take months, and even the quickest climbs take hours. This means that there are endless opportunities to stop, to say "enough!" or to slack off. Ueli did not slack off but showed us what true courage looks like—and that what follows courageous action is life lived more freely.

Ueli came in for more than his fair share of criticism. Most of it, I believe, was rooted in insecurity. People didn't believe anyone could do what he did. Their fears or limitations were too great to allow the possibility of his level of achievement. Some could not justify the risks he took. Either way, such thinking disregarded what it took Ueli to achieve his mastery and ignored his years of apprenticeship. Failing to see this, one cannot see the beautiful in the dangerous, cannot accept the risk undertaken safely, with understanding and mastery.

Wouldn't it have been wrong for Ueli to have pulled up short, to have turned away, to have allowed greatness to gather dust on a shelf in the name of playing it safe? I believe that it *would* have been wrong and also that we would have been poorer without his story.

What about the risks of high-level climbing? Taking risk entails judgment, and that means making decisions, sometimes life and death decisions, and usually with imperfect information. Climbing is not mathematics. It's simply not possible to be certain and right all of the time, and all alpinists know this. Ueli definitely knew it, and he lived with that knowledge. This doesn't make risk-taking right or wrong, good or bad, or selfish or benevolent. It simply is what alpinism—and life—is made of.

We tend to create a false sense of security in our everyday lives and to believe we're in control. We tell ourselves that we are going to live to be ninety and die peacefully in our sleep, surrounded by loved ones. But the world I've known is not usually like this. It is unpredictable, far more ruthless, and much more tragic. It is also, however, more beautiful and inspiring.

When climbers go into the mountains, we don't have in mind that we will become rich or famous. We climb to transform ourselves. A serious climber has to really want to change into an unknown future self and must seek this change tenaciously and in the face of fear, at the risk of seeming foolhardy to others. Most of us are afraid of change, especially of changing ourselves. But if one achieves this and survives one's transformational quest, no matter how quixotic it seems, revelations abound. Great journeys—not only to mountain summits—entail profound lessons. We learn that we are not static. We can change, our choices are many, and we can become someone new.

We need people like Ueli to inspire us, and we are better for having had his example. Ueli showed us what it means to live one's dreams. He was a hero and still entirely human. While I long admired him for his strength and determination, in more recent years it was his humility I found so endearing. He was vulnerable with people, something that requires a rare strength and sensitivity. It is the fully human Ueli who provides a model to help us deal with our own puny fears.

Ueli Steck shaped the sport of climbing for the better by seeing what was humanly possible and then achieving it. Benevolent leadership by good example is rare in today's fractious world. It is something few ever accomplish. Ueli was that kind of leader.

Thank you, Ueli. We can never repay you. Or perhaps we can—by following your example.

Steve House
September 2017

TRANSLATOR'S NOTE

"Climbing is like walking on stairs. I never expect to slip and fall. Do you?" This was Ueli Steck's response to my asking him how he could not be scared when scaling such gigantic, steep faces without a rope. From that moment I understood where Ueli was coming from.

I first met Ueli in 2005. I was assisting Miss Elizabeth Hawley, the renowned Himalayan archivist, when he returned from his attempt of the Khumbu Express—he had succeeded on the North Face of Cholatse and the east face of Tawoche but failed to reach the summit of Ama Dablam. Back then he was still coming to Nepal as a carpenter, the profession he made a living with, and not many people knew of him. However, it was already clear that this young man was driven. Like other climbers I interviewed for Miss Hawley's Himalayan Database, he wanted to climb difficult routes or big faces, but his goal wasn't simply to be the best or gain the international recognition that followed. Instead he yearned to explore mountains and push the physical boundaries of possibility.

Over the years I got to know Ueli well, since meeting with Miss Hawley or me was always part of his itinerary when in Nepal. Ueli was never in Kathmandu for long, with just time enough to sort out his gear and climbing permits and have a pizza at Thamel's Fire & Ice, his favorite restaurant. I remember when he came back from Everest with Tenji Sherpa, his friend and regular companion. The pair stood on the summit at 1:30 p.m. on May 18, 2012, and Ueli and I had coffee together at his hotel the following morning, just before he caught a plane back to Switzerland. He was fast at whatever he did.

Ueli was always helpful and made time to talk with me, be it for the Himalayan Database or for my job as a journalist. I was still working for a Swiss news portal, and Ueli's achievements were always a worthy story. I remember well the dispute with the Sherpas on Everest in 2013. I was at Base Camp myself that year, since I was attempting Nuptse. After the "brawl" hit the news, I received that dreaded phone call from my editor, asking me whether I would be willing to interview Ueli. I did not want to bother Ueli with this; by now he was more than just a subject for a good story, he had become a friend. But still, I was and am a journalist at heart, and so I went to see him. At first he declined, but in the evening he came over to our camp and said that he trusted me and was willing to talk to me. I really appreciated it, and the interview crystallized how shaken and traumatized he was by the whole event.

In 2014 I shared a base camp with Ueli and his wife, Nicole, when Ueli was on the ill-fated summit push with the Double 8 expedition on Shishapangma in which an avalanche killed two people. I could hear the trembling in his voice when he radioed down to base camp, and I could feel his absolute desperation and frustration that he was unable to do anything to save the lives of his friends.

Whenever we met we would talk about a possible English version of one of his books, which he really wanted to have. When I visited Ueli and Nicole in Ringgenberg in January 2017, Ueli excitedly told me that finally his latest book would be published in English. I felt very honored when he said that I would be the right person to do the translation. We contacted Mountaineers Books, and they agreed. I started working on *Ueli Steck: My Life in Climbing* in March that year.

▲ ▲ ▲

On April 30 I was translating away in a friend's garden in Dushanbe, Tajikistan, where I had a work assignment after having spent the pre-monsoon climbing season in Kathmandu. I was fully immersed in Ueli's ascents and emotions when I received a message from Monica Piris, a good friend and doctor working on the north side of Everest, telling me about Ueli's fatal fall. Sitting there with Ueli's words in my hands, I felt dizzy and lost.

From that instant the meaning of Ueli's book and my role in translating it changed. Initially I felt unable to continue. The book somehow seemed irrelevant. What was the point of it now that Ueli would no longer be able to hold it in his hands? How could I carry on without being able to ask him questions? Would the publishers want me to rush the book to get it out? It turned out that the editors of Mountaineers Books were very understanding, telling me that if I needed more time I should take it. I appreciated their concern, but after a few days of my own grieving it became clear to me just how important it was to fulfill Ueli's wish to tell his story in English and, in doing so, to share it with many more people. Although the meaning of the story had changed and the work of translation had become more emotional, I reconciled with what Ueli would have wished, and I continued.

As the translator I did my best to retain Ueli's voice and emotions. During the last month of translating, his words kept reverberating in my head: "I never expect to slip and fall. Do you?" Unfortunately, on April 30, 2017, the stairs became fatal for him.

▲ ▲ ▲

I would like to thank my friends Suzy Conway and Viv Neville for proofreading and improving my English in places; and I thank my friends and family for bearing with me over the last three months and understanding that I was completely captivated by this work. I would also like to thank Mountaineers Books for giving me the chance to tell Ueli's story to an English-speaking audience. It is the story of an amazing climber and humble person who lived his dream and showed us that sometimes it is good to step out of our comfort zone. Thanks, Ueli, for being such an inspiration. You are missed.

Billi Bierling
Dushanbe, June 2017

ABOUT THE AUTHOR

Born in Langnau in the Swiss Emmental in 1976, Ueli Steck was considered one of the world's most accomplished extreme mountaineers. At the young age of seventeen, he had already mastered 9th grade climbs. At eighteen, he climbed the North Face of the Eiger and the notorious Bonatti Pillar in the Mont Blanc massif. He later set a speed record in climbing the three big north faces in the Alps. In 2005, after he soloed two Himalayan peaks in twelve days, the German climbing magazine *Climb!* voted him one of Europe's top three alpinists. Ueli scaled Gasherbrum II, his first 8000-meter peak, in 2009 and made an ascent of Mount Everest, without bottled oxygen, in 2012. In the summer of 2015, he scaled all eighty-two of the 4000-meter peaks in the Alps—in just sixty-two days.

Ueli received the Eiger Award (in 2008) and the Piolet d'Or (the "Oscar of Mountaineering") twice: once in 2009 and again in 2014. Ueli's most recent plan was to be the first person to succeed on the Everest–Lhotse traverse, but he took a fatal fall on Nuptse in the Himalaya on 30 April 2017.

ABOUT THE CO-AUTHOR

Born in 1966, Karin Steinbach spent her childhood years in Munich; she felt at home in the mountains from a young age. During her fifteen years working for a Swiss publishing house, Karin acquired, developed, and edited many mountaineering books and edited the works of numerous alpinists. In 2001, she moved to St Gallen in Switzerland, where she now lives and works as a freelance journalist, author, and editor. She has co-authored the biographies of Ines Papert, Peter Habeler, and Gerlinde Kaltenbrunner (*Mountains in My Heart*, Mountaineers Books 2014), as well as a history on women's mountaineering. She collaborated with Ueli Steck on his three books: *Speed*, *8000+*, and *Ueli Steck*. Karin's articles on Ueli's impressive climbs have appeared in newspapers and magazines.

ABOUT THE TRANSLATOR

Billi Bierling was born in the German ski resort of Garmisch-Partenkirchen, but took up climbing only after she moved to England. She now lives in Nepal, working for the Himalayan archivist, Miss Elizabeth Hawley, interviewing expeditions about their climbs. Billi has scaled several 6,000- and 7,000-meter peaks, as well as five of the 8000-meter peaks. She is a trained translator and journalist.

LEGENDS AND LORE SERIES

THE LEGENDS AND LORE SERIES honors the lives and adventures of mountaineers and is made possible in part through the generosity of donors. Mountaineers Books, a nonprofit publisher, further contributes to this investment through book sales from more than 800 titles on outdoor recreation, sustainable lifestyle, and conservation.

We would like to thank the following for their charitable support of Legends and Lore:

FOUNDERS CIRCLE
- Anonymous
- Tina Bullitt
- Tom and Kathy Hornbein
- Dianne Roberts and Jim Whittaker
- William Sumner
- Doug and Maggie Walker

With special appreciation to Tom Hornbein, who donates to the series all royalties earned through the sale of his book, Everest: The West Ridge.

You can help us preserve and promote mountaineering literature by making a donation to the Legends and Lore series. For more information, benefits of sponsorship, or how you can support future work, please contact us at mbooks@mountaineersbooks.org or visit us online at www.mountaineersbooks.org.

MOUNTAINEERS BOOKS

MOUNTAINEERS BOOKS is a leading publisher of mountaineering literature and guides—including our flagship title, *Mountaineering: The Freedom of the Hills*—as well as adventure narratives, natural history, and general outdoor recreation. Through our two imprints, Skipstone and Braided River, we also publish titles on sustainability and conservation. We are committed to supporting the environmental and educational goals of our organization by providing expert information on human-powered adventure, sustainable practices at home and on the trail, and preservation of wilderness.

The Mountaineers, founded in 1906, is a 501(c)(3) nonprofit outdoor activity and conservation organization whose mission is "to explore, study, preserve, and enjoy the natural beauty of the outdoors." One of the largest such organizations in the United States, it sponsors classes and year-round outdoor activities throughout the Pacific Northwest, including climbing, hiking, backcountry skiing, snowshoeing, bicycling, camping, paddling, and more. The Mountaineers also supports its mission through its publishing division, Mountaineers Books, and promotes environmental education and citizen engagement. For more information, visit The Mountaineers Program Center, 7700 Sand Point Way NE, Seattle, WA 98115-3996; phone 206-521-6001; www.mountaineers.org; or email info@mountaineers.org.

Our publications are made possible through the generosity of donors and through sales of more than 800 titles on outdoor recreation, sustainable lifestyle, and conservation. To donate, purchase books, or learn more, visit us online:

**MOUNTAINEERS
BOOKS**

1001 SW Klickitat Way, Suite 201
Seattle, WA 98134
800-553-4453
mbooks@mountaineersbooks.org
www.mountaineersbooks.org

OTHER TITLES YOU MIGHT ENJOY FROM MOUNTAINEERS BOOKS

Call of the Ice
Simone Moro
"This book is among the very best reportage from the 'nearly impossible' that we have."
—David Stevenson, *American Alpine Club Journal*

Night Naked
Erhard Loretan
"One of the finest memoirs ever written by a mountaineer."
—David Roberts

Conquistadors of the Useless
Lionel Terray
"Lionel Terray takes triumph and death in his stride, a dedicated professional writing with the gusto of an amateur."
—Paddy Monkhouse, *The Guardian*

Mountains in my Heart
Gerlinde Kaltenbrunner
Effusive, charismatic, and tough, Gerlinde Kaltenbrunner climbed the fourteen 8000-meter peaks without supplemental oxygen or high-altitude porters.

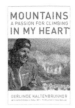

Extreme Eiger
Peter and Leni Gillman
The definitive account of the first direct ascent of the Eiger's North Face—one of the greatest and most controversial climbs of the twentieth century—written by a journalist who was on the scene.

www.mountaineersbooks.org